"About time Warren wrote a branding book. He's been the master, the visionary walking the branding walk for many decades. I founded the Starlight Children's Foundation, and decades ago, Warren founded Starlight Canada. I saw firsthand how Warren fronted the emotional promise of Starlight into its branding, the high opportunity for massive empathy by making a sad, seriously ill child happy. In making that promise to volunteers and donors, Warren branded absolute kindness and the eyes of the children as the billboard of Starlight, which rapidly became the fastest-growing children's charity. I directly copied his methods in the United States, and it was just as powerful here. Millions of Starlight children have benefited from Warren Kornblum's expertise in marketing. You can too."

—*Peter Samuelson, philanthropist, film producer, and author*

NOTES FROM THE BRAND STAND

Thoughts on Emotional Branding from Someone Who Has Fought for Consumer Attention and Won

Warren Kornblum

SGP

SHADOW GROUP PUBLISHING

Delray Beach, Florida

For permission requests, contact:
Shadow Group Publishing, LLC
warren@ShareOfHeart.com
http://ShareOfHeart.com

Project Management by Marla Markman, MarlaMarkman.com
Cover Design and Interior Design by Glen Edelstein,
HudsonValleyBookDesign.com

Ordering Information:
Special discounts are available on quantity purchases by corporations, associations, and others. For details, contact the publisher at the email above.

Publisher's Cataloging-in-Publication Data

Names: Kornblum, Warren, author.
Title: Notes from the brand stand : thoughts on emotional branding from someone who has fought for consumer attention and won / Warren Kornblum.
Description: Includes index. | Delray Beach, FL: Shadow Group Publishing, 2026.
Identifiers: LCCN: 2025921953 | ISBN: 979-8-9934262-1-1 (hardcover) | 979-8-9934262-0-4 (paperback) 979-8-9934262-2-8 (ebook)
Subjects: LCSH Branding (Marketing) | Consumer behavior. | BISAC BUSINESS & ECONOMICS / Consumer Behavior | BUSINESS & ECONOMICS / Marketing / General
Classification: LCC HD69.B7 K67 2026 | DDC 658.827--dc23

Printed in the United States of America

You Are My Inspiration

A career is built through years of experience, but it is also shaped by the people who influence who you are. I couldn't have written *Notes from the Brand Stand* without the individuals who have crossed my path and left their mark. They are key influences in my life and in the success I've achieved. Whether they're with us or looking down from heaven, they inspire me, and I hope they feel the depth of my gratitude.

To Tricia, your steady support through life's ups and downs has been a constant source of grounding and everything I need.

To my family and friends, I appreciate your steadfast support throughout my journey.

In loving memory of my parents, Phil Kornblum and Shirley Pollock, and my sister, Jaye Kornblum-Rea—your love, strength, and faith in me live on in every word of this book.

To the clients and collaborators who trusted me with their ideas, your support helped turn these thoughts into something tangible and meaningful.

And for everyone who believed in me, even when I didn't fully believe in myself, your encouragement helped give these notes their voice.

Finally, thank you, the reader, for your curiosity and for caring about what brands can achieve when made with heart. I hope this inspires you to create something that truly matters.

Contents

Introduction

I HAVE SPENT MOST of my career building brands—some large, some small, some iconic, and others just starting out. I've sat in boardrooms, brainstormed in coffee shops, stood on retail floors, and paced hallways of creative agencies, searching for the right words, the right message, and the right spark.

Over time, it became clear that three things were evident:

1. Marketing is about selling, while branding concentrates on building connections.
2. The best brands prioritize building trust instead of just grabbing attention.
3. Ultimately, you can't build a lasting brand unless it resonates with people and evolves with them.

This book offers a collection of ideas, stories, lessons, and truths I've collected over the years.

As I explore various concepts and ideas in the coming pages, I've highlighted brands I've worked with, along with my perspective on examples of other brands I admire from afar that have created niches for themselves and built strong emotional connections with their customers.

Some are legacy brands, some are contemporary, and others are start-ups. But all these brands believe in and uphold the power of strong positioning and fulfilling their promises.

There are also examples of brands that lost their Brand Stand and, along with it, their once-strong position.

From a personal perspective, I served as the chief marketing officer for Toys "R" Us during its peak years and also recognized the early warning signs of its eventual decline. Luckily, I was already gone before it happened.

Brands like Toys "R" Us, Kodak, Sears, Sharper Image, Radio Shack, Blockbuster, and many others are examples of once-dominant companies that failed because their Brand Stands didn't adapt to changing times or because they lost touch with their audiences.

Developing, understanding, and nurturing your Brand Stand at every stage of your journey is what builds, sustains, and keeps category leadership alive as your brand's future evolves.

It's what I've seen succeed, and I hope it inspires you to reevaluate the real essence of branding and what it should be.

Over the past few years, I've often been asked why I've never written a book. The truth is, I didn't want to write another marketing manual or a boastful memoir. The world doesn't need another list of tactics or a history of old campaigns.

But I kept noticing something troubling: Even as tools, platforms, and analytics improved, many brands were struggling to find their way. Leaders had tremendous access to metrics, but the statistics alone were not providing a full perspective of their customers and potential customers. While the data provided a sterile look at where they stood in the market, it didn't replace the need for instinctive and inspirational go-to-market strategies. Quarterly research had replaced conversations that once focused on belief and connection.

And yet, I've also seen the opposite. I've noticed small, resourceful teams with fewer resources achieve extraordinary success because they understood one thing: Brands live and die in the human heart. They knew how to matter to people, not just market to them. That's what brought me back to writing—because in a time when everyone's trying to be louder or faster, we need to remember how to be more human.

This book isn't a step-by-step guide or a highlight reel. It's a conversation drawn from real boardroom debates, late nights with creative teams, and lessons learned in the field—sometimes through success, sometimes through failure. It's about the part of branding you can't automate or A/B test: having the courage to stand for something meaningful and to keep proving it every day.

If you've ever felt overwhelmed by the noise of modern marketing or unsure if your brand still matters, you're not alone. I hope these pages remind you that brands are more than just campaigns and logos. They are promises, beliefs, and emotional connections that need care and conviction.

Notes from the Brand Stand is my way of sharing what decades of leading and advising brands have taught me—not as strict rules but as sparks to ignite your thinking.

At its core, a brand embodies promises. Real people decide if those promises are trustworthy. Still, it's the people behind the brand who ultimately determine whether those promises are fulfilled.

A brand is the heartbeat of a business. It keeps the blood flowing and brings everything to life.

For as long as I can remember, I have wanted to build a career in marketing and advertising. I have always been drawn to outstanding creative work and the impact of marketing on standing out and establishing connections.

Over the years, I've kept notes—lessons from the field, sharp reminders, quick truths, and emotional triggers. I've used them as tools, sparks, and sources of insight throughout my career. Some have shaped strategies, while others have helped me get through each day.

This book distills those notes, shaped by experience and refined by instinct. If any of these ideas inspire you to think differently or help you solve a problem, I'll be proud. If you walk away with several new insights, that's great. And if reading this book motivates you to develop your own ideas, that's a success, too.

Whether you're a CEO, chief marketing officer, founder,

student, or someone striving to make your efforts more meaningful, I hope these pages provide you with something valuable—something genuine, human, and memorable.

Thanks for showing up.
Let's get started!

Chapter 1
The Brand Stand
Every Brand Needs a Stand

A BRAND STAND IS your unapologetic truth—the belief that grounds your purpose, shapes your voice, and guides your decisions. It's not a slogan. It's not a mission statement displayed in the lobby. It's what you stand for, even when it's inconvenient. It's the standard you uphold, even when no one's watching.

Over the years, I have attended numerous leadership meetings where executives are divided on a bold decision—some support taking a controversial stance aligned with the company's founding values, while others worry about losing market share.

In that moment, someone calmly reminds the room, "This is why we exist. If we abandon it now, what do we really stand for?" That choice may cost short-term wins, but it strengthens a brand's identity forever.

Every great brand needs a stand. It's not just about what you say—it's about what you show the world through actions, consistency, and conviction. It's how your brand claims space in people's lives in a way that feels authentic, not forced.

Nike's "Just Do It" isn't just a phrase—it's a statement of purpose. It shows that anyone, anywhere, can become an athlete if they have the will. Sephora doesn't just sell beauty products—it promotes inclusivity with an expanding range of shades, training programs, and cultural awareness. Liquid Death doesn't just hydrate—it challenges you to join a counterculture movement against plastic waste, humorously packaging water in metal cans.

These brands aren't just selling products—they're selling belief systems.

In today's crowded and competitive world, a Brand Stand is more important than ever. It cuts through the noise by providing clarity. It offers your team clear direction and gives your audience something to believe in. It's your flag in the ground—and you wave it not just during good times but especially during tough ones.

But too many brands play it too safe. They test constantly, seeking approval instead of making a real impact. They develop strong positioning statements but then hide them away. They're afraid of alienating anyone, so they end up standing for nothing memorable.

Imagine a brand that tries to please everyone—uses bland and overly tested language, has no clear point of view, and creates products that copy competitors. They avoid risks, so they never make anyone rethink or even notice the brand. They run advertising campaigns, but customers can't tell what the brand truly stands for.

In a crowded marketplace, this kind of safety seems invisible. Without a stand, no message gets through.

I learned early in my career how risky that can be. One of the first moments that shaped my thinking happened during a campaign review with a client named Harry Saunders, who managed marketing and advertising for Jack Fraser, a major Canadian men's wear retail chain. We were presenting new, creative, safe, strategic, and well-executed work. Harry leaned back, paused, and said:

"This is good, but I was hoping to see something that would make my palms sweat."

He wasn't aiming for shock value. He wanted work that evoked genuine emotions—something authentic and bold. That phrase stayed with me throughout my career. It reminded me that if you're not a little uneasy with your brand's boldness, then you're probably not saying anything that truly matters.

I've often argued that playing it safe is one of the riskiest moves a brand can make. Safety feels secure—it avoids criticism, keeps stakeholders comfortable, and creates an illusion of stability. But in truth, safety gradually stifles belief.

I've sat in boardrooms where brands tried to hedge their bets, watering down every decision to avoid offending anyone. The result? Campaigns no one remembered, messages no one repeated, and products no one bragged about.

True stands don't come from consensus—they grow from conviction. Conviction means making decisions that evoke emotion, even disagreement, because people eventually understand who you are and what you stand for.

The most enduring brands don't ask, "Will this upset someone?" They ask, "Will this matter and resonate with the people who believe in us?" That's an entirely different perspective, and it's where courage begins.

A Brand Stand defines your boundaries. It clarifies what you will pursue and what you will walk away from. It communicates to employees what to prioritize and to customers what to expect. It creates alignment—and when executed effectively, it inspires admiration.

Steve Jobs famously told his team, "We will only build insanely great products." That wasn't just marketing—it was a manifesto. It served as a filter for every product decision and set expectations for every Apple customer. It also showed the team what was worth fighting for.

Authenticity isn't something you can outsource. You can hire the best agency in the world, have killer creative, and spend millions on media—but if your brand doesn't know who it is, it will always feel empty.

That's the difference between borrowed interest and true belief.

And belief, unlike attention, can't be bought. It's the most human of all brand metrics. Belief turns customers into more than just buyers—they become advocates.

Imagine a dinner table debate where someone criticizes a brand you truly believe in. Loyal customers won't stay silent; they'll passionately share stories about what that brand means to them, how it performs, and how it makes them feel appreciated more than others in the same category.

That's not marketing—it's conviction shared between people and brands.

It lives in people's hearts and shows when they support you without being asked, forgive your mistakes, and proudly stand with your purpose. It's what turns a purchase into a relationship—and a customer into a believer.

To earn that belief, you need to stand firm on your principles.

It's easy to say you care about innovation, sustainability, or inclusion. It's much harder to turn those values into action. That's where true credibility comes from. Brands like REI don't just post about environmentalism—they've built their entire co-op model around it. They give employees "opt-outside" days. They showcase diversity in marketing and store staff. They demonstrate their commitment to the beliefs they promote.

Another example is Patagonia. They've long supported environmental justice—and they don't just use that message to sell jackets. They've sued the US government over land conservation. They've transferred ownership of the company to a trust that funds climate causes. That's a Brand Stand that shows up in policy, not just marketing.

Want to see what happens when a stand is faked? Just look at brands that "go woke" only during Pride Month or tout sustainability while producing mountains of plastic. Consumers are savvy. In a world of receipts, screenshots, and instant backlash, hollow claims swiftly backfire.

So, how do you determine your Brand Stand?

It starts with honesty. You should ask sincere questions—not about marketing but about meaning.

- What sets our brand apart?
- What conviction would we hold onto, even if it costs us?
- What change are we tired of waiting for?

These questions go beyond strategy; they reveal your core values. Once you answer them honestly, you'll begin to understand the foundation of your stand.

Your Brand Stand isn't meant for everyone. It shouldn't be. The most compelling stands attract both supporters and skeptics. They clearly show who you're for—and who you're not. That's not exclusion. That's honesty.

Great brands don't chase consensus. They set the direction with clarity. Costco didn't try to be all things to every shopper. They built a membership model that rewards loyalty with unmatched value. Their Brand Stand is based on trust and consistency, clearly showing who they serve and reminding everyone that belonging has meaning and benefits.

Spotify didn't just offer access to music—they transformed it into a personal experience, curating playlists that reflect moods, tastes, and identities. Their Brand Stand is about connecting through curation, making each listener feel like the music was made just for them.

Glossier didn't aim to be just another traditional beauty brand. They created a community centered on real skin, real people, and a simple aesthetic. They didn't wait for permission; they welcomed participation.

Ooni didn't just sell backyard pizza ovens. They sparked a movement, encouraging people to share recipes, experiments, and family traditions. Their Brand Stand is clear in their tone, customer service, and the love their community shows every day.

A strong Brand Stand requires consistency. If you claim to care about something, it should be evident in your hiring, packaging, messaging, partnerships, and customer experience. Every action must support this stance. If it doesn't, people will notice—and they won't forgive the gap.

A Brand Stand holds you accountable while also empowering you.

When you demonstrate belief, clarity, and courage—when your actions align with your values—your brand becomes memorable. It builds loyalty that can't be faked and relevance that can't be bought.

And one more thing: A Brand Stand isn't fixed. As the world evolves, your values shouldn't— but how you express them can. Brands that last aren't the loudest or trendiest. They are the ones that grow with purpose and adapt without losing their core.

Great leaders realize that a brand's stand isn't fixed but rooted in purpose. As the world evolves, you might need to adjust how you communicate your position without losing its core. Think of it like tuning a compass to steer through storms—the direction stays steady, but the route shifts.

Brands that revisit their stand with clarity create resilience that endures for generations.

Because when a brand genuinely embodies something—and clearly shows it—it doesn't just sell more. It matters more.

And in a noisy world, that's the kind of brand people remember, believe in, and support.

The Brand Stand is the foundation of everything. But simply taking a stand isn't enough—you need to make people feel something genuine. Winning loyalty today isn't about louder messages or clever campaigns. It's about creating an emotional bond strong enough to outlast every competitor's offer.

The Heart of the Matter

The strongest Brand Stand can be conveyed in a single breath, in a way no one else can claim. Here are a few to think about:

- *Costco:* Great value for members
- *Glossier:* Beauty shaped by community
- *Ooni:* Restaurant-quality pizza made at home
- *Patagonia:* Prioritizing the planet
- *REI:* Prioritizing purpose over profit
- *Spotify:* Every playlist reflects who you are

Chapter 2
Building Emotional Loyalty
Feelings Win Hearts

BRANDS DON'T JUST SUCCEED because they're useful; they succeed because they're meaningful. Beyond awareness, convenience, and price, there's something deeper that separates the brands people use from the brands they love.

That something is emotional loyalty.

It's that feeling of "This brand gets me. It reflects me. It values me. It means something to me."

When emotional loyalty exists, a brand transforms from being just an option to the only choice. It's not only about product specs or dashboards; it's about the feelings that linger long after the transaction concludes.

Emotional loyalty depends on trust, which is developed through shared values and reinforced by meaningful moments that make people feel seen, understood, and appreciated.

It's easy to dismiss emotion as too soft or difficult to measure. But emotion is the most powerful force in branding. It's what transforms a passive customer into a passionate believer. Today, people want to know not just what your product does but also what you stand for—and how you make them feel when they use it.

Think about a time when you chose a brand that wasn't the cheapest, fastest, or even the technically best. Maybe a competitor offered more features or a better deal, but you selected the one you felt most connected. That pull doesn't appear on a product spec sheet. It comes from moments that made you feel seen—experiences that fostered trust in the brand beyond logic. That's the invisible thread of emotional loyalty. Once it's woven in, it's difficult to undo.

When you win someone's heart, you also gain their loyalty and support. And their wallets tend to follow.

Loyalty Is Rooted in Emotion, Not Logic

Brand love isn't rational—it's emotional. Algorithms don't govern it. It's about how someone feels when they think about, talk about, or interact with your brand.

Features and benefits attract attention. But emotions like trust, pride, identity, joy, and belonging are what create a real connection.

We remember the brands that make us feel something. The ones that enter our conversations and daily routines. We choose them not because we have to but because we want to—because we'd miss them if they were gone.

You know you've built emotional loyalty when people can't quite explain why they love you—but they feel it.

Beyond Metrics Toward Meaning

It's tempting to measure connection using data: click-through rates, loyalty points, A/B tests. But real emotional bonds don't always appear in a spreadsheet.

They exist in small, intentional gestures—remembered preferences, caring service, the right message at just the right moment. A return policy that prioritizes people over procedures and a voice that feels like a friend, not a form letter.

These things don't scale easily, but they build trust exponentially.

A brand that feels human earns something no algorithm can replicate: trust.

One of the strongest signs of emotional loyalty is when customers remain loyal even after a mistake. For example, a retailer once sent the wrong product to a loyal customer. Instead of just sending a generic apology email, the owner personally called, composed a handwritten note, and gave a free gift along with a promise to improve.

The customer told friends not only about the mistake but also about how genuine and caring the response felt. Emotional loyalty builds when a brand shows it will support customers through problems, not just when everything goes well.

These are the moments people remember and share.

Marketing Is an Act of Caring

When done properly, marketing isn't manipulation—it's compassion. It involves engaging with empathy, listening without judgment, and crafting messages that reflect your stand and genuinely resonate.

It's about treating customers not just as conversions but as individuals who want to feel heard and respected.

And when you genuinely care—truly care—people notice. They respond to it. They talk about it. They come back. They might even bring friends.

When emotional loyalty is strong, customers not only keep coming back but also defend your brand. If you've created a genuine emotional bond, your customers become true advocates. They share personal stories that numbers can't measure. That's emotional currency in action—a trust so deep that customers are willing to risk their own credibility to vouch for you.

Transaction vs. Transformation

Most brands focus on the transaction. The discount. The deal. The CTA.

But the truly great ones strive to transform. They say, "You belong here. We understand you. This will make you feel better. This will make your life easier."

Emotional loyalty isn't developed at the checkout screen. It's built through moments before and after. Each moment provides an opportunity to reinforce or diminish the connection. Every detail matters.

From Awareness to Relevance

Being known is no longer enough. You can buy awareness, but relevance can't be purchased.

Relevance is something you earn.

It's the difference between being recognized and being remembered. It's what makes people choose you, even when faster, cheaper, or newer options are available.

Brands that foster emotional loyalty are consistent, authentic, and reflect the values of the people they serve. They don't just tick boxes—they create meaningful connections.

They follow through. They walk their talk. They keep their promises and show their humanity.

Emotional Loyalty Is a Valuable Brand Asset

Prioritizing emotional loyalty means you're not just acquiring customers but also fostering long-term commitment.

And in today's world, commitment is rare.

But when you have it, you don't just close the sale. You tell a story. You become part of someone's life. You become the brand they not only use but also believe in.

Emotional loyalty gives your brand staying power, but loyalty can't survive without purpose. A brand without a reason for being will eventually become just another option.

This is why emotional loyalty lasts longer than campaigns, trends, or even leadership changes. Products may change. Teams might rearrange. Markets can shift. But when people truly believe in your brand—when it becomes part of who they are—they remain loyal. They'll forgive slow shipping, accept a price increase, and even follow you into new categories or businesses because the connection runs deeper than a single transaction. That's when loyalty shifts from just a marketing goal to a part of someone's life story.

The most potent brands lead with purpose—absolute, authentic conviction—not just a marketing trend or seasonal campaign.

The Heart of the Matter

- **People might try a product for its features, but they stick with it because of feelings.**
- **Consider what your customers would miss—not just lose—if your brand vanished tomorrow.**
- **Loyalty develops when a brand offers a sense of belonging, not just a product to purchase.**
- **What emotional promise do you offer each day that makes leaving you difficult to consider?**

Chapter 3
Purpose Is Essential
Purpose Drives Relevance

PURPOSE HAS BECOME ONE of the most overused words in business today. It's displayed on walls, included in slide decks, featured in campaigns, and repeated at leadership summits. At first glance, that might seem like progress—companies finally recognizing they need to stand for something bigger than just transactions.

But look closer, and you'll notice something's missing.

The issue isn't that brands talk about purpose. It's that too many treat it like a slogan—something to say, not something to prove. They craft lofty mission statements, post heartfelt videos, and then return to business as usual. Nothing truly changes. Purpose becomes mere decoration. When that happens, customers and employees immediately feel the disconnect.

Purpose, when misused, becomes performative. And performative purpose erodes trust.

The Dangers of Saying Without Doing

People are more perceptive than ever to authenticity. They can tell the difference between a brand that acts with conviction and one that's just following trends.

We've all seen the campaigns: emotional music, poetic narration, a bold promise to change the world. But when the experience doesn't match the message, people don't just tune out—they call it out. They question everything the brand claims. They grow skeptical. Cynical.

That's why performative purpose causes more damage than saying nothing at all. A brand that claims values but doesn't live up to them loses credibility faster than one that stays silent.

You don't earn points just for playing the game. You gain trust by living your truth.

Purpose Is a System, Not a Statement

A true brand purpose isn't something you invent in a workshop. It's not a headline, a presentation, or a marketing asset. It's the core focus of your business—the reason why decisions are made the way they are.

It's how you hire. It's how you prioritize. It's what fuels innovation, shapes culture, and enhances customer experience. It's embedded, not announced.

You know a purpose is genuine when taking it away would dismantle the entire organization. That's how deeply it should be ingrained in the business.

It's not about being perfect; it's about being consistent, accountable, and willing to choose purpose over convenience when the moment calls for it.

Real Purpose Is Built for the Long Term

Short-term tactics always tempt us—flash sales, marketing stunts, quick wins. But purpose operates on a different timeline. It's not meant for this quarter. It's designed for the next decade.

The most resilient brands—those that withstand disruption, leadership changes, and cultural shifts—are built on something more fundamental than just margin or growth targets. They have a core. A guiding compass.

Purpose provides you with that. It keeps you grounded when the market fluctuates. It gives your team something to rely on when the numbers are down. It invites customers to stay with you when options become louder or cheaper. Because when your brand stands for something meaningful, people don't just shop with you—they believe in you.

And belief lasts longer than any promotion.

Living Your Purpose Isn't Always Easy

Here's what's often misunderstood: Purpose isn't soft. It's not comfort food. Real purpose will push you.

Sometimes it means walking away from revenue that doesn't align. Turning down a partnership that looks great on paper but doesn't reflect your values. Redesigning your supply chain to meet your sustainability claims, even when it hurts your margins. Being willing to take a public stand on an issue because it matters, even if some customers disagree.

That's what distinguishes genuine purpose from seasonal marketing. It's not what you say when it's easy. It's what you do when it's hard.

And yes—sometimes it will cost you. But the price of abandoning your values is far greater.

Purpose Begins and Ends with Leadership

You can't delegate purpose to a department. It's not the marketing team's job or just a slide in a board presentation. It belongs to and relies on leadership.

Because purpose reveals itself in decisions—especially the quiet ones. The ones that never garner a press release.

When leaders make choices that align with the brand's stated values, people notice. Employees start to trust. Culture begins to align. Customers feel the difference in every interaction. And when leaders break that alignment—when they talk a big game but compromise at the first sign of pressure—everyone notices that, too.

Culture isn't determined by the brand book; it mirrors the behavior of those in charge.

If the leaders at the top don't embody the purpose, it's not genuine.

Be Honest Before You Attempt to Be Inspirational

Another trap: attempting to craft the perfect purpose statement.

Many brands aim for poetic, grandiose language—talking about saving the planet, changing the world, making life better for everyone. But when those claims aren't supported by real actions, they fall flat. Or worse, they become targets.

You don't have to sound like a nonprofit to have purpose. You don't need to change the world to matter. You just need to mean what you say.

Begin with honesty. Purpose comes from truth, not aspiration.

You can't achieve integrity through marketing. But you can earn it—by taking action, being transparent, and showing progress.

Where Purpose Shows Up

If your purpose is genuine, it won't need explanation—it will be felt:

- **In your culture:** Do employees feel empowered to act on your values? Are they rewarded for doing the right thing, not just hitting the numbers?
- **In your products:** Do innovations bring you closer to your mission or just follow trends?
- **In your experience:** Do customers feel your values through how they're treated, how your product is delivered, and how your team presents itself?

When purpose is genuine, it appears in the details. It's not just a slogan—it's a behavior.

When You Get It Right, Everything Comes Together

Purposeful brands don't just foster loyalty. They generate momentum. Employees feel linked to something greater than their daily tasks. Customers identify with your story. Stakeholders become collaborators in something meaningful.

That's when branding becomes more than just messaging. That's when a brand begins to matter—not only because of what it sells but because of what it stands for.

And that's when trust develops. Trust enables you to try new things, grow, make mistakes, and still be forgiven because people believe in the "why" behind what you do.

A Warning About Borrowed Purpose

One of the most common mistakes I see? Borrowing someone else's purpose. Latching onto trends like sustainability, inclusion, or mental health because they're culturally relevant, not because they reflect who you truly are.

Don't do it. You'll never own it. Even worse, you'll lose credibility by trying.

You don't have to address every issue. Just stand firm on what's true to you. That focus builds clarity, and clarity breeds confidence.

Customers aren't seeking perfection. They're seeking honesty. Give them that—and keep proving it—and they'll follow.

The Heart of the Matter

- **If your marketing suddenly disappeared tomorrow, would your customers still understand what you stand for?**
- **Purpose isn't just a slide in a deck. It's what people experience from you every day— especially when no one's watching.**
- **Don't try to prove everything all at once. The most effective changes often begin with small steps. Focus on one part of your business where your purpose can be demonstrated through action—and let that truth speak louder than any campaign. For instance:**

  » *Show people you care about the planet.* **Reduce waste and choose long-lasting, eco-friendly packaging.**
  » *Show up for your community.* **Focus on people and places, not just ads.**
  » *Show everyone they belong.* **Incorporate genuine diversity into your products and stories.**
  » *Show employees they matter.* **Offer small benefits that have a big impact.**

Chapter 4
Brand Gravity
Great Brands Pull You In

SOME BRANDS ATTRACT YOUR attention without you knowing why. You notice them once, then again, and suddenly they start to feel like part of your life. You find yourself thinking about them, talking about them, and considering them even when you're not actively shopping for their products. That's not just recognition—that's gravity.

Brand gravity isn't about having the loudest voice or the most significant media budget—you can buy awareness. But gravity is different. Gravity doesn't push—it pulls. It attracts people naturally through a force that feels genuine, earned, and difficult to ignore.

Think about the last time a brand subtly caught your attention. Maybe it was a small restaurant you passed by every day before finally stopping in, or a running shoe that you kept seeing people wearing until you felt compelled to try it.

These aren't coincidences. They're early signs of gravity—the feeling that a brand belongs in your life, even before you consciously decide to let it in. This force grows quietly, pulling you closer one moment at a time until choosing that brand feels as natural as breathing.

What Gravity Feels Like

For a customer, gravity seems effortless. They aren't thinking about why they're attracted; it just happens. The brand begins to feel familiar. It feels safe. It becomes part of how they navigate their world. Over time, that pull becomes automatic—a default choice, even when new options emerge.

This isn't magic—it's behavior. People naturally tend to trust what feels consistent and emotionally relevant. When a brand acts in ways that reduce uncertainty, boost comfort, and reinforce identity, it becomes easier to choose. That feeling of "ease" is gravity at work.

I once worked with a brand that had a brilliant product hidden beneath layers of complicated options and confusing instructions. Customers liked the idea but hesitated because every interaction felt like a puzzle. They felt like they had to buy more to get what they wanted.

When we simplified the process—fewer choices, clearer language, easier navigation—something changed. People spent more time on our site, not less; sales increased, and customer satisfaction scores rose.

There's no doubt that making the exploration and purchase process simpler boosts appeal. When a brand eliminates friction, confidence takes its place.

The Power of Pull

When a brand successfully builds loyalty and establishes a meaningful relationship with its customers, it becomes less about encouraging people to shop and more about consumers feeling drawn or "pulled" toward the brand.

The more we engage with a brand—and the more those interactions are positive—the more it feels safe and comfortable. Repetition builds confidence, not boredom. A brand that consistently shows up reliably creates a mental shortcut: "This is the safe choice."

When experiences are intuitive and seamless, they not only appear efficient but also feel right. People naturally prefer options that require less effort.

We are attracted to brands that mirror who we are or who we want to be. Buying from them lets us express ourselves. The connection gets stronger when choosing a brand feels like selecting someone or something we know and trust, instead of just picking anonymous products.

Observing others engage with or speak positively about a brand boosts its influence. We tend to prefer brands that have built a following, and we feel confident knowing that the people we notice and are influenced by support those brands. This collective backing creates momentum—a sort of cultural wave that makes the brand even more difficult to ignore.

When these forces align, a brand no longer needs to forcefully push its message into every space. Instead, the pull of trust, relevance, and recognition does the work.

How Gravity Builds

Gravity doesn't happen overnight. It develops gradually, with each interaction strengthening a brand's pull. Think of it as a four-stage process:

1. **Initial awareness:** This is the spark—the moment you first encounter the brand. Advertising, public relations, or word of mouth can introduce it to you, but at this

stage, it's only an impression. Curiosity might bring you closer, but you're not yet fully engaged.

2. **Emotional connection:** A moment happens that shifts your focus from merely noticing a brand to becoming genuinely interested. This marks the turning point where curiosity turns into trust. You have your first moment of confidence—small but enough to make you think, "I like this brand."

3. **Habitual choice:** Repetition strengthens the bond. Each positive experience reduces doubt, making it easier to choose the same brand again. You stop comparing options or shopping around; you go directly to the brand you trust. This is when the brand moves from being one of many to becoming your preferred choice.

4. **Advocacy and evangelism:** When at full strength, customers don't just return—they promote. They tell friends, share stories, and defend the brand. This advocacy is fueled by emotional momentum. The brand has reached escape velocity, effortlessly pulling others into its orbit.

Examples of Gravity in Action

Brands like On Running have built a loyal following not just because of high-performance shoes but also through storytelling and designs that connect emotionally. Their distinctive sole is instantly recognizable and has become a badge of identity, telling a story about innovation and movement that runners and everyday people wear with pride.

Canopy doesn't just sell humidifiers; they reframed them as beauty and wellness tools designed to hydrate skin and hair, not just a room. That positioning turned a utilitarian appliance into part of a self-care ritual.

Notion didn't just launch another productivity app. Its gravitational pull comes from giving people the freedom to build their own systems—pages, templates, and workflows shaped by the community. That flexibility turned users into evangelists, orbiting around a platform that feels personal and participatory.

Stanley didn't just revive a century-old thermos brand. Its charm lies in transforming a simple tumbler into a cultural icon—the Quencher as a symbol of identity and belonging. The brand's blend of durability, design, and community pride attracted people, making carrying one not just practical but essential.

These brands didn't gain gravity by seeking attention. They developed it slowly through consistent experiences that fostered trust and emotional connections over time.

What Weakens Gravity

Just as gravity grows stronger through consistency and connection, it can weaken quickly if the forces holding it together break apart.

- **Broken promises:** When a brand fails to deliver on what it promises, even once, it damages trust.
- **Inconsistent experience:** Disjointed messaging, poor service, or unpredictable quality cause emotional friction, making customers second-guess their choice.
- **Overcomplication:** Adding unnecessary steps, jargon, or confusing options makes engagement feel burdensome rather than natural.

Without alignment between actions and values, trust weakens. Customers start to drift away, and rewinning their loyalty often takes far more effort than earning it in the first place.

Strengthening Gravity

Building and maintaining brand gravity requires deliberate, consistent efforts that build over time. However, sustaining it demands more than regularity—it calls for decisions that continually reinforce trust.

- **Show up consistently.** Every touchpoint should feel aligned with your brand's personality—unique and authentic. Consistency builds familiarity, which in turn nurtures trust.
- **Make it easy.** Remove obstacles. When your brand feels straightforward to choose or use, people naturally stick with it. Friction not only slows them down; it weakens the pull.
- **Create emotional resonance.** Emotion makes you unforgettable. When a brand taps into deeper feelings of pride, belonging, or joy, it becomes part of identity, not just a product choice.

True gravity isn't something that exists on its own within the marketing department; it is strengthened through product choices, company culture, and leadership actions. When the brand's promise is kept and respected, customers feel it instinctively without needing any prompts.

Why Gravity Matters

In today's world, where every market is crowded and every brand battles for clicks and impressions, gravity is the key to cutting through the noise. Advertising can spark interest, but gravity keeps it ongoing. It turns "I'll try it once" into "I'll buy it again" and transforms one-time buyers into lifelong advocates.

Without gravity, a brand remains stuck in perpetual acquisition—constantly pushing and spending to stand out. With gravity, the brand reaches a tipping point where customers attract others, multiplying its influence without increasing costs.

Gravity shows that a brand matters—not just because people recognize it but because they are drawn to it. It reflects emotional influence, indicating that belief has taken root.

The Heart of the Matter

- Ask yourself and your team: *What genuinely draws people to us—without promotions, discounts, or gimmicks?* If the answer feels weak, you might be forcing attraction rather than earning it.
- If it's your purpose, your unique position in the market, and the emotional connection people feel, you're creating gravity.
- If it's just another price cut, close-out, or financing trick, you're running on fumes, not loyalty.
- Genuine brand gravity is magnetic because it's authentic. It causes people to lean in, not because you shout louder but because they feel something real pulling them toward your brand.

Chapter 5
Culture Drives Brands
Values Shape Reputation

EVERY GREAT BRAND IS built from the inside out. It begins with belief—what the founders value, how the company makes decisions, and what it chooses to prioritize when nobody's watching. That belief, when shared and lived consistently, becomes culture.

And that culture becomes a fundamental support for the brand.

Far too many companies talk about culture. They describe it as fun perks or a mission printed on the wall. But real culture isn't just a mood—it's a system. It's how people act, speak, solve problems, and treat each other, especially when things go wrong.

Culture is the heartbeat of your brand. It's where your values are tested. It's where promises are made—or broken.

The Invisible Driver Everyone Senses

Customers might not see your culture directly, but they feel it. Every customer service interaction, every in-store moment, each "How can I help you?" or "Please hold"—these all reflect what's happening inside your walls.

I've seen brands with massive marketing budgets fail because their internal culture didn't match their external message. One legacy retailer I worked with had a polished brand story and huge awareness—but their internal environment was broken. Employees were disengaged, turnover was high, and leadership kept changing. Stores felt cold. Staff didn't care. Customers took notice. Eventually, they stopped coming.

The brand failed—not due to a lack of awareness but because of a lack of belief.

On the other hand, I've also seen brands where the culture was the key advantage. Employees felt empowered. They understood the mission. They believed in the product and in each other. That pride led to better service, smarter decisions, and a stronger brand image—without needing a bigger ad budget.

That's why I always say: A brand's strength depends on the culture backing it.

Culture Isn't Defined by a Deck

You can't define your culture in a memo. You can describe it. You can aspire to it. But your culture is what people experience every day—how they're treated, how decisions are made, how wins are celebrated, and how failures are handled.

It's the unwritten rulebook employees follow when no one is watching.

Culture isn't "what we say we do." It's "what actually happens here."

You can tell a strong culture by how people show up. Are they just going through the motions, or are they bringing energy? Are teams working together or competing? Do people defend the brand when it's under pressure—or pass the buck?

Great culture reveals itself during tough times.

Culture Begins with Leadership—and Radiates Out

Culture doesn't flow from slogans; it emanates from actions—especially from leadership.

Leaders influence culture daily by the standards they set, the behavior they accept, and the priorities they highlight. If leaders claim "We care about the customer" but only celebrate quarterly growth, employees will understand: Numbers are more important than people.

When leaders consistently demonstrate curiosity, integrity, and ownership, those traits become ingrained throughout the organization.

You can't outsource or delegate that. You have to experience it yourself.

Culture Is Contagious

Culture spreads rapidly—for better or worse.

When it's healthy, you can feel it: People speak with pride, treat each other with respect, and advocate for the brand. That energy reaches the customer, even if they don't realize where it originated.

When it's toxic, you feel it, too. Indifference spreads. People protect themselves instead of each other. Blame replaces curiosity. And eventually, that rot seeps into every customer interaction.

The true test of culture isn't how a company behaves on a good day—it's how it responds when things go wrong. Does the team panic or take ownership? Does it retreat or rally? In crisis, real culture shows itself.

Singapore Airlines: Culture in Action

Singapore Airlines is a clear example of how culture drives brand success. For decades, they have provided some of the highest-rated service in the world. But it's not because of the newest planes or the best food—it's because of the people.

From day one, employees are trained not only in procedures but also in perspective. They learn to see themselves as ambassadors of care. Service isn't scripted—it's a shared belief. That belief manifests in small moments: a flight attendant sensing a nervous traveler and responding with warmth, or a gate agent resolving a customer issue without needing layers of approval.

Even in an industry that often pursues automation, Singapore Airlines prioritizes humanity. Their culture isn't loud—it's felt. And customers remember it.

Don't Mix Up Culture with Perks

Culture isn't about free lunches or branded hoodies. Those are perks. Perks are nice—but they're not why people stay.

People stay for meaning. For consistency. For a workplace where values aren't just talked about in all-hands meetings but are reflected in how meetings are conducted, how decisions are made, and how people are treated—regardless of title.

If your team members don't feel trusted, respected, or heard, no ping-pong table will fix that.

Culture is the feeling people carry home at the end of the day.

What You Tolerate Becomes the Culture

Here's a tough truth: The behavior you permit reflects what you encourage. Every time a toxic high performer gets a pass, your values weaken. Every time someone cuts corners and no one speaks up, your culture shifts—quietly but noticeably.

People don't pay attention to company values on posters. They notice what leadership excuses, overlooks, or avoids.

That's why culture is shaped moment by moment, decision by decision.

You can't fake it. You can't retrofit it. You have to build it intentionally.

Inside-Out, Not Outside-In

This is where "inside-out branding" really matters. Before you focus on how customers see your brand, ensure your team truly believes in it.

I've seen too many companies launch branding campaigns before fixing their internal story. That only makes the gap more obvious. Customers see the ad, then experience something completely different in-store, on the phone, or online.

You can't create brand love on employee indifference.

Begin internally. Establish the culture properly. Ensure your team feels it—and truly believes it. Then empower them to take that conviction into the world.

Culture Is a Competitive Advantage

A strong brand culture simplifies everything.

- Recruiting becomes attractive—people want to work there.

- Customers notice the difference—and return.
- Mistakes turn into opportunities for trust, not merely damage control.

Culture isn't soft; it's strategic. It influences brand behavior long after any marketing campaign concludes.

Get it right, and marketing gets easier. Get it wrong, and no amount of marketing will save you.

The Heart of the Matter

- **Walk your floors. Listen in on meetings. Notice how people behave when no one's watching. That's your brand—right there.**
- **If your internal energy isn't aligned with your external promise, address your inner self first.**
- **Your brand is your people. Culture isn't just a line item; it's the foundation. Build it accordingly.**

Chapter 6
The Brand Experience
Feelings Define the Brand

A BRAND ISN'T JUST what you claim it to be. It's what people feel.

You can tell customers what your brand stands for. You can create the most beautiful website, write award-winning copy, and design a logo that belongs in a museum. But none of that matters if the experience doesn't match the message.

Branding exists in the details—how someone is greeted, how they are treated, and how they feel after they walk away.

Experience is where belief is formed—or shattered.

Where Branding Becomes Real

Earlier, we discussed company culture as the heartbeat of a brand. That internal belief system shapes how people behave. But experience is where it becomes visible. It's the moment when all your internal work is either confirmed or contradicted—where the customer decides whether to trust you.

And here's the tough truth: They don't judge by your messaging. They judge by their experience.

That's why the brand isn't just your campaign. It's the hold time at the call center. It's the packaging. It's how a store associate solves a problem or how your chatbot responds when someone's frustrated. These are the real moments that stay with people.

And customers remember how you made them feel long after they forget what you told them.

Promises Are Easy; Proving Them Is Harder

I've worked with companies that spent millions on rebrands—new positioning, new colors, new taglines. But the moment a customer walked into a store or contacted support, the illusion collapsed. The tone didn't match. The experience didn't live up to the story.

People notice, and when the gap between promise and delivery becomes visible, trust breaks down.

On the other hand, I've seen brands with small advertising budgets succeed because their experience spoke for itself. Every customer interaction reinforced the brand's values. The service was honest. The product worked. The tone was warm and consistent.

It didn't just build trust—it created stories. Stories that customers shared. Stories that became the core of the brand's campaign.

Experience Is Marketing

If your customer experience is outstanding, people will share it with others. If it's disappointing, they'll tell even more people.

Great brands know that every interaction matters. The return process. The thank you email. How your website makes someone feel. These moments either reinforce your promise or betray it.

That's why experience design should be regarded not just as UX (user experience) owned and managed by the operations team but as part of brand strategy. UX is the sum of every interaction that shapes how a customer feels about you.

It's not just about avoiding mistakes. It's about building connections. The best experiences don't feel transactional—they feel human.

Designing for Emotion

We usually think of customer experience as logistics—ease, efficiency, convenience. But the true magic happens when a brand builds emotional confidence. That feeling of "They thought of everything. They see me. They made this easy, and I trust them."

A hotel that remembers your name. A café that knows your order. A subscription service that makes canceling painless. These aren't just marketing tactics—they're emotional moments. Moments that say, "You matter here."

And when customers feel that, they stick around, not out of habit but out of trust.

Aman: A Master Class in Emotional Experience

Aman is one of the clearest examples of experience as a brand.

Aman is a luxury hotel brand known not for its glitz or advertising but for serenity, precision, and personal care. They rarely run ads. They don't need to; the experience does the marketing.

When you arrive at an Aman property, it's tranquil—not just in sound but in atmosphere. Staff members don't bombard you with greetings; they anticipate your needs. Your preferences are remembered, and your space feels like it has been designed just for you.

Need to shift your dinner reservation because the weather changed? Already done. Want your favorite tea after your morning swim? It appears—without asking.

Everything feels deliberate, fluid, almost invisible. And that's the point. The experience is meant to make you feel cared for, not controlled.

And the result? Loyalty and evangelism. Not because of points or perks but because of how the experience made someone feel.

Experience Is the Most Authentic Part of Your Brand

You can script ads and polish social copy, but you can't fake the genuine moment when a customer interacts with your product or team.

That's why experience is the most genuine part of branding. It's where intent becomes reality.

If you claim to be customer-first but have a confusing return process, people won't trust you. If you say you're innovative but your onboarding feels clunky and outdated, the illusion fades. That inconsistency causes doubt.

On the other hand, if the experience matches the brand promise—even subtly—it fosters confidence. You don't have to shout. You just need to deliver.

Experience It Yourself

One of the most effective habits a leader can develop is to think like the customer.

Use your website. Call your support line. Try to return a product. Read your auto-emails. Walk into one of your locations anonymously.

Don't focus on what customers say about your brand—pay attention to what they feel.

One CEO I know does this every month. She orders products through her e-commerce platform. She sends her mom to customer service. She visits her stores without wearing a name tag. Then she shares these stories in leadership meetings—not as complaints but as data.

That kind of direct immersion changes everything. It makes the conversation more authentic. It closes the gap between brand intention and customer reality.

Every Moment Counts

Experience isn't just the "customer journey." It's hundreds of small choices: tone of voice, default settings, the cleanliness of a bathroom, the kindness in a return policy, the language in a shipping delay email.

These are the places where trust is gained or lost.

It's easy to pursue innovation and overlook the fundamentals. However, customers typically just want to feel valued. They seek clarity. Simplicity. Respect.

Designing experiences around those values is how brand love grows.

Don't Mix Up Efficiency with Connection

As brands grow, there's a tendency to automate. In many cases, that's necessary. But too often, automation sacrifices warmth. Speed takes precedence over empathy. Scripted responses take the place of human ones.

Technology should enhance humanity, not replace it.

A great experience is one where technology handles the heavy lifting and people focus on the connecting. That balance creates magic. And magic builds loyalty.

The Heart of the Matter

- **If you want to understand what your brand truly represents, become a customer and experience what they feel.**
- **Every experience is an opportunity to gain or lose belief.**
- **Marketing attracts attention. Experience builds trust. Don't mix up the two.**

Chapter 7
Brands Are Built on Truth
Honesty Beats Hype

EVERY BRAND HAS A story to tell. The most compelling ones are built on honesty—an authentic, unshakable foundation that customers can sense without being told. Weaker brands have to work harder at it, covering up empty promises with gloss and marketing until the truth eventually reveals itself.

Truth is the quiet force behind belief. It's earned slowly through actions that match words, promises that are kept, and a level of transparency that makes people feel safe believing in you.

A brand rooted in truth doesn't need to shout to be heard. Customers speak for them by sharing stories about what the brand truly stands for. They believe not only in what the company sells but also in what it represents.

Messaging Isn't Meaning

Many companies stumble because they confuse messaging with genuine meaning. They believe that creating the perfect tagline or hiring the right influencer will fast-track their way to credibility. But when the experience doesn't match expectations or when internal practices clash with the company's stated values, customers leave—and worse, they tell others why they've left.

Truth isn't a marketing ploy; it's a fundamental business strategy. It should be evident in everything you do. Every part of the organization needs to reflect it. When there's alignment, customers notice it right away. When there's misalignment, they sense it even more quickly.

Patagonia: A Promise You Can See

Patagonia is a prime example of a brand built on truth. Long before sustainability became a buzzword, Patagonia's identity centered on environmental responsibility. They didn't just produce outdoor gear; they made a commitment to protect the planet and operated as if that promise was more important than short-term profit.

From donating a portion of sales to conservation efforts to famously running an ad telling people *not* to buy a jacket they didn't need, Patagonia consistently upholds its mission. We're told that its founder, Yvon Chouinard, even transferred ownership of the company to a trust dedicated to environmental causes, ensuring that profits will go toward protecting the planet indefinitely.

That authenticity didn't just build a brand—it ignited a movement. Customers became loyal supporters because they believed in the company's truth. When someone wears a Patagonia jacket, it reflects their values just as much as their style or outdoor skills.

Contrast that with brands that try or have tried to exploit sustainability as a trend. They slapped green labels on packaging, launched eco-themed campaigns, and sponsored environmental events—but behind the scenes, little changed. Once customers discovered the gap between claims and reality, those brands lost credibility overnight. No amount of PR can fix a breach of truth.

Truth in Everyday Promises

This isn't just about high-profile issues like sustainability. Truth is important in every promise a company makes. A bank that claims to prioritize customers but hides fees in fine print isn't telling the truth. A tech company that promises privacy but secretly sells data isn't truthful. A restaurant that markets itself as farm-to-table but sources ingredients from industrial suppliers isn't being honest.

Dishonesty or even less-than-truthful messaging causes more than just lost sales. It plants lasting doubts that damage a brand's reputation in people's minds. Customers remember when they feel they've been misled. They tell their friends. They're hesitant to give the brand a second chance. The brand may try to recover with apologies and rebranding, but unless the core truth changes, those efforts probably won't succeed.

Brands built on truth, on the other hand, have resilience. When they make mistakes—and all brands eventually do—they receive grace because customers know their intent is genuine. They've earned trust through years of honesty, and that trust serves as armor during crises.

LEGO: Rediscovering the Truth

In the early 2000s, LEGO faced a crisis. Sales were dropping sharply, and many wondered whether the legendary toy brand could survive. To stay relevant, LEGO pursued licensing deals, digital games, and products that strayed far from its original mission.

But something felt off to longtime fans. The brand that once stood for sparking creativity and imagination through simple building blocks was losing its way. Instead of sticking to its core values, LEGO was chasing trends.

Eventually, LEGO's leadership recognized the disconnect and took a bold step: They refocused on their core mission of inspiring creativity through hands-on play. They improved product quality, listened to their builder community, and emphasized designs that encouraged imagination.

The turnaround was remarkable. Today, LEGO isn't just a toy company; it's a cultural icon that reaches into movies, theme parks, and education—yet it all connects back to its original truth: inspiring creativity, one brick at a time.

Truth Simplifies Leadership

Truth also makes decision-making clearer. When leaders understand what's real and non-negotiable, they stop chasing every trend or competitor move. They have a clear sense of direction that points to long-term relevance, not short-term noise. Customers sense that stability. They feel they're dealing with a brand that knows itself, which makes it easier for them to understand and trust it, too.

Being a truthful brand doesn't mean revealing every company detail or being perfect. It means being genuine. It involves admitting when you fall short, explaining decisions honestly, and never pretending to be something you're not. It's choosing transparency over cleverness.

We live in an era of radical transparency. Social media, review sites, and instant access to information have removed the ability to control brand perception from the top down. You can't hide flaws in the story; customers see behind the curtain. The only sustainable approach is to embrace transparency.

The Courage to Be True

Building a brand based on truth requires courage. It's often easier to embellish or project an image of perfection or to follow the latest trends instead of facing tough realities. However, real growth happens when you confront those truths directly and align your entire company around them.

Authenticity provides another benefit: It draws the right people. Employees who believe in the brand's mission tend to stay longer, perform better, and become ambassadors. Partners who share your values strengthen your network. Customers who trust you remain loyal because they believe in you.

As we move forward in this book, we'll explore belief and emotional loyalty—how a brand moves beyond being just a product to something customers feel connected to. That change can't happen without truth at its heart. Without it, every emotional bond is fragile, and every promise is temporary.

A brand built on truth is unshakable. Competitors can copy your products, undercut your prices, or outspend your advertising budget, but they can't replicate your authenticity. That's the ultimate protection in a world where trust is scarce and skepticism runs high.

The Heart of the Matter

- **Truth has no budget, but it builds the strongest brands.**
- **Review every promise your company makes—from the website to the sales floor—and every point of contact a customer has with you, and ask yourself if it's fully, undeniably true.**
- **When truth is missing, every message is a house of cards.**

Chapter 8
Build Meaning, Not Just Attention
Meaning Fosters Loyalty

IN TODAY'S BUSINESS ENVIRONMENT, it's easy to become hooked on quick wins. Quarterly earnings calls, instant customer feedback, and real-time dashboards—they all encourage leaders to seek immediate results. Clicks, conversions, and short-term sales spikes often indicate success.

Quick results aren't the same as loyalty. A short-term win might get attention or even boost revenue temporarily, but it rarely fosters the kind of trust that keeps customers coming back.

The strongest brands resist the temptation to only play for today. They know that loyalty develops gradually, through consistency and trust—not through short-term artificial wins.

The Sweet Temptation of Short-Term Wins

I've seen companies celebrate a surge in sales after a promotional blitz, only to watch the numbers drop sharply once the sale period ends.

Short-term tactics don't build lasting relationships; they only provide temporary incentives to customers. Relying heavily on promotions can be a double-edged sword. They work while they're active, but once they end and you haven't developed a loyal customer base, potential customers just wait for your next deal.

Businesses that fall into this trap train their customers to wait for discounts, doing nothing to strengthen brand trust.

True loyalty is about making customers feel confident choosing you again and again—even when you're not on sale or the most convenient option. It comes from delivering fair value and fulfilling or hopefully exceeding their expectations when shopping with you. That requires patience and courage, especially when everyone else seems focused on immediate results.

Why the Mattress Industry Was Ripe for Change

For decades, the mattress industry stayed the same—big brands relied on brand recognition, retail distribution, and the belief that consumer buying habits would remain constant. Then new direct-to-consumer brands like Casper, Nectar, and Purple recognized an opportunity. They addressed customer frustrations, such as confusing pricing, pushy sales tactics, and a lack of transparency. By modernizing the shopping experience—making it simpler, more accessible, and clearer—they quickly became very popular.

Suddenly, long-standing leaders like Serta, Sealy, and Simmons began to be the challengers. They weren't toppled solely by better products but also because they failed to adapt to shifting consumer expectations.

The lesson is clear: Believing your brand has the "right" to lead because of past success is risky. Markets shift. Customers evolve. If you don't adapt, someone else will change the rules—and make you seem outdated in the process.

Tesla: Playing the Long Game

Some brands take a different route. Tesla, for example, didn't build its reputation through flash sales or big discounts. Instead, it gained loyalty by consistently focusing on a mission: speeding up the world's transition to sustainable energy.

In its early years, Tesla faced production delays, public skepticism, and significant controversy. Many companies in that situation would have used aggressive tactics to attract investors and customers. Tesla took a different approach. It focused on innovation—investing heavily in technology, infrastructure, and software updates that kept the company at the forefront of automotive technology.

People are attracted to Tesla because they feel they're not only adopting cutting-edge technology but also joining a larger movement: a cleaner, more sustainable future. That kind of loyalty doesn't weaken with promotions; it grows stronger over time.

Amazon: Investing Beyond the Quarter

Amazon demonstrates long-term thinking. Jeff Bezos famously stated that Amazon's decisions are made with a multi-year outlook. While competitors focus on quarterly profits, Amazon invests in infrastructure, delivery networks, and customer convenience—actions that often hurt short-term profits but ultimately build strong customer loyalty.

Millions of people now choose Amazon not because of occasional deals but because they trust it to deliver every time. That trust wasn't bought with coupons; it was built through years of consistently proving reliability and value.

Loyalty as a Cultural Commitment

There's a misconception that loyalty is passive—that if you're good enough, people will naturally stick around. In reality, loyalty is actively earned and protected over time. It demands constant attention to detail, unwavering focus on providing value, and a willingness to resist easy wins that could damage credibility.

In earlier chapters, we discussed culture and truth. Those principles are important here because you can't build lasting loyalty without them. A strong culture keeps you focused on what matters most, even when you're tempted by short-term gains. Truth makes sure that the promises you make today still feel honest tomorrow. Together, they form a foundation that short-term tactics can't shake.

One of the challenges leaders face is pressure—appropriate pressure from investors, boards, or even employees—to deliver results in real time. This pressure can be suffocating, and it's understandable why many surrender to it. However, the brands that endure find ways to balance accountability with patience. They clearly communicate a long-term vision and invite stakeholders to buy into it, helping everyone see that true success is judged not just by this quarter's figures but by the strength of relationships built over years.

Short Term or Long Term? A Simple Test

Here's a practical way to think about customer loyalty: Imagine that every customer interaction has an invisible expiration date. If the action builds loyalty that outlasts the campaign itself, it's long-term brand-building. If the result disappears as soon as the promotion ends, you've just paid for a sugar high.

The best leaders constantly ask: "Does this decision make us more trusted in a year? Five years? Ten?" If the answer is no, even a significant short-term gain might be a long-term mistake.

The Rewards of Patience

The reward for playing the long game is substantial. Loyal customers spend more over time. They forgive occasional missteps. They recommend you to others not because you asked them to but because they genuinely want to. Loyalty compounds—it turns buyers into believers, believers into advocates, and advocates into a living extension of your brand.

There's nothing wrong with seizing opportunities when they come up. The issue starts when quick results become the main goal instead of focusing on consistently doing the right things. Brands that only chase short-term gains often burn out, while those that stay true to a bigger vision tend to succeed in the long run.

Every leader must decide: Focus on short-term results, or build for a strong future. You can do both if you keep perspective. Building long-term loyalty may take more time and feel more challenging, but it offers resilience that no competitor can easily take away. In a marketplace full of noise and fleeting attention, loyalty is the rarest—and most valuable—currency you can earn.

The Heart of the Matter

- **Ask yourself which decisions you're making solely for speed—and whether those choices will still be logical a year from now.**
- **Focus on the future your brand aims to create, not just the goals to reach this month.**
- **If you prioritize trust and consistency now, the results will follow—and unlike quick wins, those results will be lasting.**

Chapter 9
Brand Belief
Belief Lasts Longer than Products

EVENTUALLY, SOMETHING CHANGES.

A customer purchases your product for practical reasons: It satisfies a need, the price is right, and the timing lines up. It's a straightforward transaction—nothing more, nothing less. But then something unexpected occurs.

The product exceeds expectations. The support is friendly. The follow-up feels personal. It doesn't just deliver—it connects. The customer doesn't feel like a number—they feel seen.

And from that moment on, they don't just come back because it's convenient. They come back because it feels right. You've become their first choice—not just a choice.

That's when a brand shifts from being just about products to becoming something customers believe in.

More than Loyalty

This isn't just about loyalty or preference. Belief runs deeper. It's emotional, not logical. It's not about what the brand does—it's about what the brand represents.

Belief is what causes customers to choose you even when competitors offer better deals or faster shipping. It's what encourages them to defend you in conversation. It's what transforms brand users into brand advocates, even evangelists.

Belief transforms a transaction into trust, a product into a story, and a purchase into a relationship.

The Anatomy of Belief

Belief develops gradually but intentionally:

- **Trust comes first.** You keep your promises consistently.
- **Then comes appreciation.** You go beyond expectations in genuinely human ways.
- **Then comes alignment.** The customer begins to see their own values reflected in yours.
- **Then comes belief.** They stop shopping around, talk about you, and invite others to join in.

At that point, you're not just a brand they use; you're a brand they believe in.

And belief is one of the strongest forces in branding—because it keeps people loyal even when logic suggests they should leave.

The Moment When Belief Takes Hold

Belief isn't always loud; it often comes in quiet moments.

- A customer gets a handwritten note after a purchase—and recognizes that someone cared.
- A shipping delay is managed with such grace and responsibility that the inconvenience vanishes.
- A company makes a public mistake—but responds

with such transparency that trust grows, not diminishes.

These moments aren't easy to scale, but they are incredibly important. They serve as the emotional proof points people carry with them. When belief starts to form, it's rarely because of your ads; it's usually because of what someone experienced—and how it made them feel.

Belief Starts Within

You can't establish belief from the outside if it isn't present inside. Belief begins with your team.

If your employees don't believe in the brand—what it represents, how it functions, how it treats people—customers will sense the disconnect. You can't overcome it just through marketing. Belief can't be faked.

That's why belief is an inside-out process. The people behind the brand must feel it first. That conviction flows through the product, the service, the tone, and the touchpoints. Only then does it reach the customer.

And when customers sense it, they don't just respond—they reciprocate.

What Belief Looks Like

You'll know you've built belief when customers do things you didn't ask them to do:

- Defend you in a comment thread
- Recommend you to a friend without being prompted
- Create content or reviews for others—not for perks but because they genuinely want to

They might display your logo on their laptop, share your story on a podcast, or insist that their friend "just has to try" your brand.

That kind of advocacy isn't incentivized—it's inspired.

Belief is what transforms a customer base into a community and, in rare instances, into a movement.

Nike: From Product to Purpose

Nike exemplifies belief in action. "Just Do It" was never just about sneakers—it was a challenge, an identity, a mindset.

People wear Nike because it symbolizes something: drive, effort, determination, and possibility. Nike has built that belief over decades—not just through athletes and sponsorships but by consistently aligning with stories of resilience and self-expression.

Not everyone agrees with every Nike campaign. That's part of the point. Belief isn't built by appealing to everyone. It's built by standing for something that certain people deeply care about.

When a brand becomes a belief, people don't just buy it. They wear it. They defend it. They live it.

Canada Goose: The Badge of Belief

Canada Goose is another example—less flashy but equally rooted in truth. Outerwear originally created for Canada's toughest climates, the brand became a symbol of function, authenticity, and craftsmanship. Over time, it also became a symbol of identity.

When someone wears Canada Goose, they're not just keeping warm. They're communicating something about themselves— what they value, how they see the world, and their beliefs about performance, design, and durability.

That's belief in action: when a product turns into a symbol.

Belief Builds Resilience

Belief is what sustains your brand during uncertainty.

In tough times—supply-chain issues, leadership shifts, PR problems—brands built on belief tend to bounce back faster. Not because they're perfect but because people give them the benefit of the doubt.

Belief grants you grace. It earns you patience. It provides space to course-correct without sacrificing your community.

That type of resilience can't be bought. It must be earned.

Belief Cannot Be Forced

One common mistake I see is trying to engineer belief solely through marketing.

It doesn't work.

You can promote your values and showcase your commitment. However, belief is always a customer's decision. It's granted, not taken. It's based on what people observe, not what you claim.

And once lost, it's nearly impossible to win back.

That's why belief is sacred and should never be taken for granted.

You Become Part of Their Story

When belief takes hold, you're no longer just a brand on a shelf. You become a part of how someone sees themselves:

- The runner who wears your shoes to train for their first marathon
- The parent who trusts your car seat to keep their child safe

- The young professional wearing your brand to their
first big interview

In these moments, belief transforms branding into identity. The brand becomes part of someone's story. They didn't just purchase from you—they brought you into their life.

That's not only powerful. It's lasting.

The Heart of the Matter

- **Has your brand become part of someone's story— or are you still just selling things?**
- **When people believe in you, they no longer need convincing. They begin bringing others along.**
- **Belief arises from honesty, consistency, and care. Build that—and your brand becomes more than what you sell.**

Chapter 10
Human Brands Win
Connection Is the Advantage

WE LIVE IN AN era of artificial intelligence, automated services, and algorithm-driven everything. Machines can mimic nearly anything now—voices, images, even empathy. But when technology seems able to replicate humanity, it's the brands that are truly human—empathetic, present, and trustworthy—that stand out.

Being human is no longer just a nice-to-have. It's a competitive advantage.

Human brands don't just transact; they connect. They don't shout, "We care!" They demonstrate they care through their actions. They're not trying to sound human; they inherently *are* human—in their decisions, actions, and accountability when things go wrong. And we often process them in our minds just as we would real human beings.

Humanity Starts Inside

A company can't pretend to be human in public if it isn't practiced privately. The way leadership listens to and values team members sets the tone. Human brands start by treating their people with dignity and trust. When employees feel heard and appreciated, they pass that same care to customers.

Honesty in the Hard Moments

Every brand will eventually encounter a difficult moment: a defective product, a security breach, a service outage, or a crisis outside anyone's control. What defines a brand in those moments isn't perfection—it's presence.

When something goes wrong, human brands don't hide; instead, they speak openly. They respond quickly, transparently, explain what happened, and share how they are fixing it. They admit mistakes without hiding them in fine print or scripted apologies.

Customers don't expect you never to stumble; they expect you to care enough to stand with them when you do. Vulnerability isn't weakness—it's proof that real people are behind the logo.

Invisible Friction, Visible Humanity

We've all experienced the dehumanizing effects of poorly designed systems. Things like:

- Entering a sixteen-digit account number, then repeating it to three different representatives
- Being transferred from department to department to fix something simple and having to repeat yourself every time
- Dealing with a chatbot that misunderstands questions and provides irrelevant knowledge links
- Being directed to an FAQ that doesn't directly relate to the issue you're trying to address

These aren't just operational flaws—they're breaches of trust.

When efficiency takes precedence over empathy or when cost-cutting removes the human element, customers don't just feel inconvenienced—they feel invisible. And invisibility undermines loyalty.

Human brands challenge that narrative. They focus on dignity. They consider what it's like to be on the other side of the screen or counter. They don't just track speed; they track relief. They ask: "Did we make this person's day easier, calmer, and more supported? Did we respect their time because it is one of the most valued things consumers desire?"

Moments That Matter

Human connection doesn't always stem from grand gestures. Often, it's the tiniest, simplest actions that make the biggest impact. These moments don't grow easily, but they grow loyalty.

I once advised a brand during a product recall. The usual corporate approach would be to release a safe statement, automate refunds, and hope the issue gradually fades away.

Instead, the CEO delivered a clear, heartfelt message, taking responsibility for the mistake. The company doubled its support staff so customers could speak to real people who were ready to listen and assist. The recovery was costly in the short term, but customers remembered the sincerity long after the issue was resolved.

That experience boosted the brand's reputation more than ten years of campaigns ever could.

Four Seasons: A Human Standard

Few brands embody human connection better than Four Seasons Hotels and Resorts. Known for luxury, it isn't chandeliers or lavish amenities that make it legendary—it's the way employees make guests feel.

Every staff member is empowered to resolve issues without needing multiple approvals. It's the little details that make a difference. Showing compassion and appreciation is part of their culture. Initiative is rewarded, and complacency is frowned upon. It's all about the guest, and the guests appreciate it.

These aren't just corporate policies—they're initiatives that foster human responses, based on trust that employees understand how to care for people in real time.

Four Seasons doesn't have to boast about having compassion or going beyond the norm, or showcase outstanding guest relations stories. Exceptional service and attention are simply part of who they are.

Guests show their loyalty through their trust, helping build a reputation that emphasizes thoughtful, human touches instead of perfection. Competitors may copy luxury decor or pricing, but few can match the authentic feeling of caring for guests.

This is humanity as a strategy. It turns a hotel stay into a lifelong relationship, where guests keep coming back not only because they love the properties but also because they believe in the people behind them.

Knowing When to Hold Back on Automation

Technology is amazing for solving routine problems. Automation can reduce wait times, speed up checkout, and send reminders that no human could possibly manage.

But technology can't feel.

When the stakes are high emotionally—when a customer is frustrated, anxious, or hurt—what they need most isn't efficiency; it's connection. During those times, being directed to a chatbot or receiving a templated response feels like abandonment.

The most human brands recognize when to let technology step back. They use digital tools for tasks that don't need empathy so that human energy can focus on what matters most: building trust and resolving emotional stakes.

This isn't about inefficiency—it's about building loyalty. People remember when you look them in the eye, listen to them, and treat them as more than just a customer service ticket to resolve.

Humanity Earns Emotional Safety

Customers seldom define loyalty through "great automation." Instead, they describe feeling secure with a brand. This sense of safety comes from knowing that promises will be kept, that fairness outweighs fine print, and that when trouble arises, someone will have their back.

That's why the most human brands succeed—not because they're perfect but because they're dependable and empathetic. They make people feel like they matter.

And emotional safety is nearly impossible for competitors to copy. Price can be matched. Features can be duplicated. But the feeling of being seen and understood? That belongs only to the brand that earns it.

The Shift Toward Listening

Human brands don't guess. They listen—actively and continuously. They don't fear complaints; they welcome them as insights. Every interaction becomes an opportunity to understand and improve.

When customers perceive this transparency, trust deepens. Instead of feeling like they need to compete for attention, they feel welcomed into the brand's growth. That changes everything. Growth stops being about persuasion and shifts focus to the relationship.

The Heart of the Matter

- Do people see you as friends or just a place they go to get stuff?
- Notice not only what works but also how it feels.
- A truly human brand offers more than just functionality—it provides emotional safety. Competitors can match your prices or copy your features, but they can't easily replicate the feeling of trust you've built.
- Make your brand feel authentically human and reliably safe.

Chapter 11
Lead with Listening
It's the Heart of Communication

IN A WORLD WHERE every brand is shouting louder, faster, and flashier, the real competitive edge belongs to the brand that knows when to stay silent and listen.

Listening isn't passive—it's an act of leadership. It demonstrates humility, respect, and emotional intelligence. It indicates that your brand isn't made for people but built with them.

I worked with a start-up facing loud, well-funded competitors. Instead of trying to match their advertising budgets or outshout their messages, the founder chose a more subtle approach.

He spent hours in customer forums, direct messages, and support calls—just listening. In a relatively short time, he identified patterns that no market report had revealed and introduced features customers didn't even realize they wanted. While competitors flooded every channel with marketing messages, this brand quietly built trust. Listening became its most powerful growth tool—outperforming every loud megaphone in the market.

The best brands aren't those with the loudest voices. They're the ones with the sharpest ears—brands that make customers feel heard long before they feel sold to.

Listening as Brand Behavior

Most people view branding as what a company communicates—campaigns, taglines, bold announcements. But listening is also a form of branding. It might be the most human way a brand can show up.

Spotify didn't dominate streaming by guessing what people wanted. It quietly observed behavior—what users played, skipped, and replayed—and adapted based on those patterns. This wasn't just data analysis; it was a way of listening that influenced playlists, recommendations, and even new product features.

Notion is an all-in-one productivity app that allows users to create their own workspace for notes, projects, and collaboration. It didn't grow by flooding channels with ads or spam. Instead, it grew by listening. Every feature and update reflected what its community requested. Its forums and social spaces became more than just support desks—they demonstrated that user voices influence the product. This connection made people feel like co-creators rather than just customers.

BarkBox, a customized toy and treat subscription service, succeeds not just because of cute packaging or convenience but because it listens carefully. It notices when a dog prefers a certain toy or when a subscription needs adjustments, and it adapts without customers having to say a word. Those small, thoughtful gestures speak louder than any marketing message ever could.

In each of these instances, listening isn't just a support function—it's a strategic advantage. It changes guesswork into relevance and transforms transactions into relationships.

The Four Stages of Listening

Not all listening is the same. Many companies believe they're listening just because they gather feedback or conduct surveys. Authentic listening develops through stages, each one fostering more trust and connection.

Stage 1: Hearing

Most companies collect input—customer emails, survey results, social comments—but rarely take action on it. That's where most organizations stop. Dashboards fill up, but decisions stay the same. Hearing alone can create a false sense of connection, often frustrating customers when they see no response to what they've shared.

Stage 2: Understanding

At this stage, brands interpret feedback for deeper meaning instead of just recording it. They look for meaning beneath the words.

A telecom executive I once worked with blamed rising churn rates on pricing. But through in-depth listening—sitting in on customer interviews—we discovered that customers weren't upset about cost. They felt abandoned after purchase. They loved the product but craved better support. The solution wasn't to slash prices—it was to improve post-sale care.

Understanding turns feedback into empathy. It's the difference between logging issues and feeling what customers experience.

Stage 3: Acting

Listening becomes powerful only when it sparks change. Policies need to shift, products should evolve, and experiences must improve because of what you've heard.

Figma is an excellent example. The web-based design platform succeeds not because of top-down commands but due to its community-driven feedback cycles. Users often see their suggestions implemented in updates, along with transparent notes explaining the changes. This approach turns users into collaborators instead of just consumers.

Stage 4: Proving

The final stage occurs when listening transforms into belief. Customers see that their voices are heard and acted upon and that the brand values this process.

Proving happens when:

- Updates are clearly communicated with "You asked. We delivered."
- Suggestions are acknowledged, and credit is given to the customer.
- Changes are lasting, not quick fixes that fade.

Once a brand reaches the proof stage, customers start to see themselves as co-creators. They feel proud of helping shape the brand. That pride is hard for competitors to break because it's personal.

Listening Builds Trust

Trust isn't built by just telling people you care. It's built when they see you paying attention to what matters to them.

When they feel truly heard, they engage more. They forgive mistakes because they trust you'll fix them. They remain loyal because leaving would be like ending a relationship—not just walking away from a vendor.

Listening humanizes technology. It turns personalization from creepy or mechanical into something warm and thoughtful. It builds emotional safety—the feeling that, even when problems arise, you're in a conversation with someone who respects and understands you.

Leadership Sets the Tone

Listening starts at the top. Leaders decide whether it's just a formality or a core value. Teams mirror what they observe. When leaders dominate meetings, suppress dissent, or avoid tough conversations, employees tend to do the same with customers.

Conversely, when leaders encourage dialogue, take time to consider various viewpoints, and respond openly to feedback, listening becomes embedded in the culture.

Great leaders understand that silence can be a powerful tool. They leave space in conversations for others to speak, resist the urge to fill every silence with their own solutions, and create environments where truth feels safe to surface.

I've sat in boardrooms where this kind of leadership completely transformed a company's energy. When executives focused on listening—especially to frontline employees—ideas surged, morale improved, and internal trust directly led to better customer experiences.

The Ripple Effect of Listening

True listening not only boosts customer satisfaction scores but also strengthens the entire organization. Products improve because real-world pain points guide development. Experiences become smoother as frontline feedback helps refine processes. Messaging resonates because it's based on authentic conversations, not corporate assumptions. And culture becomes stronger when people realize that ideas matter more than titles.

Not long ago, I advised a company where a midlevel employee had been quietly suggesting a change to the onboarding process for over a year. Leadership never heard about it until a new CEO opened forums for feedback. That single idea, finally put into practice, drastically reduced staff turnover and increased employee satisfaction.

Listening speeds up innovation not by rushing decisions but by focusing resources on the most important issues. Brands that listen stop merely reacting and start acting with clarity and purpose.

A Quiet Competitive Edge

Listening is how brands differentiate themselves without shouting. Competitors may copy products, match prices, and imitate campaigns, but they can't easily replicate deep listening relationships built over years.

Listening creates a gravitational pull. Customers don't just remember what you sold them—they remember that you understood them. When competitors try to lure them away with louder messages or temporary discounts, that bond keeps them anchored.

True listening is where trust begins. But trust only lasts when it's supported by credibility—when customers see consistent proof that their voices matter. That's the next step for any brand serious about loyalty: turning what you've heard into clear, lasting action.

The Heart of the Matter

- **Listening isn't just waiting to speak—it's making necessary adjustments because you understand.**
- **Challenge yourself to excel at quiet leadership.**
- **Listening builds connection, reduces tension, and strengthens loyalty.**
- **When customers and employees feel heard, your brand's voice naturally becomes more effective—and its credibility is undeniable.**

Chapter 12
Deliver on Promises
Credibility Is Earned, Not Claimed

EVERY BRAND MAKES PROMISES, but the best ones follow through consistently and continually.

In a world where attention spans are short and skepticism runs high, proving what you say has become the most valuable currency in branding. A bold tagline or slick campaign might catch someone's eye briefly, but trust is only built when actions consistently align with words.

Why Proof Outshines Hype

Modern customers are relentless critics. They can instantly compare reviews, share experiences publicly, and spot inconsistencies with a single online search.

That creates a risk for brands if they exaggerate or make flashy promises without substance, causing customers to hesitate and doubt. When the gap between words and actions widens, it not only costs a sale but also harms long-term trust.

You can buy attention, but you can't buy credibility. Proof is the link between what you say and what people believe.

Small Signs, Big Trust

Proving your promise isn't always about grand gestures. Sometimes, it shows up in small, quiet signals that accumulate into belief over time.

It's orders that arrive when you said they would. Support teams that follow up after resolving an issue. Products that work exactly as advertised, with no surprises. Or honest updates when plans change, delivered with transparency instead of spin.

Each of these conveys a clear message: We deliver on our promises.

Once people experience that, they stop shopping for alternatives and become part of your brand's family. Trust makes them return automatically because they know what they'll get, and that security is hard to walk away from.

Stages of Proof

Belief through proof is very important, but it doesn't happen overnight. It develops in stages.

Stage 1: Promises Without Proof

Many brands start with bold claims to grab attention but offer little proof to back them up. Awareness might go up, but trust does not. Customers might try the product once but aren't necessarily willing to buy again without considering other options. You still need to work to earn their confidence.

Stage 2: Consistent Delivery

In this stage, brands begin consistently meeting expectations. Packages arrive on time. Support remains dependable. Products perform as promised. Confidence increases, but it remains delicate.

Stage 3: Proactive Proof

This is where the shift occurs. Brands no longer just meet expectations—they surpass them in ways that are noticeable. Updates are delivered before customers ask. Quality checks are transparent. Communication feels like reassurance rather than explanation.

FedEx is a prime example. Its promise—"When it absolutely, positively has to be there overnight"—is more than just a slogan; the company built an entire logistics system to fulfill that promise every day. From real-time package tracking to highly disciplined delivery operations, FedEx didn't just claim it could deliver—it proved it so consistently that customers based their own businesses on that dependability.

Proof like that doesn't depend on marketing—it turns into marketing. Customers share the story for you because they've experienced your fulfilled promises.

Stage 4: Reputation as Evidence

When proof becomes habit, it evolves into reputation. Customers recommend the brand based on personal experience. Competitors can spend millions trying to win them over, but trust is already established.

Consider Costco. Its promise is simple: great value, fairness, and quality. For decades, Costco has demonstrated this through practices like a famously generous return policy and products that prioritize member trust over quick profits. Shoppers understand that one of Costco's main goals is to take care of them. This commitment builds legendary loyalty: Costco members don't just like the store; they believe in it.

Turning Mistakes into Proof

No brand is perfect. Mistakes happen, but mistakes also present opportunities to build credibility.

Handled properly, a single resolved mistake can build more trust than a hundred flawless transactions. Customers remember how you respond when things go wrong—that's when they learn whether they can truly rely on you.

From Claims to Operational Truths

Promises are easy to make, but proving them requires integrating them into the way you do business.

If you promise simplicity, your processes must truly be easy to navigate. Or if you promise innovation, your teams must consistently challenge the status quo by bringing new ideas to the forefront. And if you promise extraordinary customer care, every employee must have the authority and resources to deliver it.

You can't market your way past a weak foundation. A proof-driven brand starts by aligning every system, decision, and detail with its promises. That alignment ensures customers experience your values in action, not just hear about them but actually see them in practice.

Leadership's Role in Proof

Leaders establish whether a brand is known for bold claims or reliable actions. Proof-driven leaders:

- **Make genuine promises.** Leaders avoid the temptation to overpromise for temporary attention. They commit only to what they can reliably deliver.
- **Invest in delivery.** They dedicate resources to systems, tools, and training that guarantee promises are kept—even under pressure.

- **Reward follow-through.** Teams are recognized for the operational excellence that customers experience.
- **Be accountable.** When leaders admit mistakes and explain how they will improve, it sets the standard for everyone else.

Great leaders understand that belief can't be forced. It's earned over time through consistent proof—and it vanishes instantly if broken.

Proof Builds Emotional Safety

People don't just choose brands logically. They choose them based on feelings. They want to feel safe from disappointment, confusion, or betrayal. Proof provides that security. It reassures customers that you can count on us. We'll keep our word.

Feelings of emotional safety foster habits. Habits generate loyalty. Loyalty drives advocacy.

When proof is strong, customers don't just believe your words—they live by them. They tell others, "This brand does exactly what it says." That advocacy is priceless because it comes from experience, not marketing spin.

Keep Promises Carefully.
Prove Yourself Relentlessly.

In a competitive market, it's tempting to promise more than you can deliver. But each unfulfilled promise chips away at credibility.

The strongest brands follow a different path. It's not just about attracting with the promise; it's more about the appeal of keeping the promises.

They make sure their promises are selective and sincere. They understate when necessary, trusting that actions will speak louder than words ever could. They focus on operational truth rather than marketing bravado.

Over time, this restraint builds in your favor. A brand that consistently shows its value no longer needs to persuade as long as it keeps proving itself. It has gained a reputation for earning customers' trust one interaction at a time.

The Heart of the Matter

- **Are you consistently keeping the promises you make?**
- **Pick one promise that feels unfinished, and go out of your way to keep it. Don't twist or alter it— just follow through.**
- **Every broken promise spreads quickly. Every fulfilled promise builds trust that no competitor can steal.**
- **Trust isn't based on words—it's established through proof.**

Chapter 13
The Brand Is Everywhere
Every Action Matters

YOUR BRAND ISN'T LIMITED to a campaign, logo, or most recent social media post.

It's in the product someone unboxes, the email you send after the sale, the tone of your return policy, the vibe your store gives off—even the way your employees talk about the company when they think no one's listening.

In today's world, your brand is everywhere, whether you manage it or not.

It's not just what you say—it's what people experience, observe, and remember.

And the most successful brands understand this. They act like living beings: consistent, purposeful, and aligned in every interaction.

Brands Are No Longer What You Say They Are

Once upon a time, you could define your brand with a 30 second TV commercial. You controlled the message. You spoke, and the audience listened.

That world no longer exists.

Today, your brand is shaped by what others say about you—what they post, share, review, or whisper to a friend. Your official message still matters, but it's just one voice in a much bigger conversation.

People encounter your brand in moments you never see—through user reviews, customer forums, behind-the-scenes TikToks, support threads, Reddit comments, employee Glassdoor posts, and even the secondhand opinions of someone else's bad experience.

You're no longer just shaping perception. You're actually living within it.

Every Touchpoint Tells a Story

Whether you mean to or not, your brand is constantly communicating:

- How your customer service team manages frustration
- Your website's speed (or slowness)
- The attitude of a store associate on a quiet Tuesday
- The tone of a shipping notification
- The appearance of your packaging
- The layout of your physical spaces
- The ethics involved in your partnerships
- The style of your job postings

All of it influences how people perceive who you are.
And everything either builds or destroys trust.

You Can't "Turn Off" the Brand

Many companies see the brand as just a department—something owned by marketing. They launch a campaign and call it brand-building. But your brand doesn't clock out when the ad ends. It doesn't pause when the campaign wraps up. It doesn't wait for the next brainstorm.

It's always active. Which means that everything is part of the brand.

- The way you handle mistakes? **Brand.**
- Your internal voice? **Brand.**
- Your founder's online behavior? **Brand.**
- Your supplier decisions? **Brand.**
- How you treat job applicants? **Brand.**

In a world of radical transparency, there are no neutral zones. Every action, every choice, and every voice contributes to how you're perceived—and felt.

Your Team Is Your Front Line

Often, the strongest or weakest part of your brand is the people representing it. Your frontline employees are your brand ambassadors, whether you call them that or not.

They are the ones your customers interact with most directly. How they present themselves matters because people don't separate the product from the person. If your product is excellent but the person delivering it is apathetic or rude, the brand fails in that moment.

That's why your internal culture is closely connected to your external brand. You can't expect employees to provide exceptional brand experiences if they don't feel empowered, valued, or respected.

Internal energy influences external behavior.

Your brand enters the room every time your people do.

Behavior Is the Brand

It's easy to get caught up in brand guidelines, tone-of-voice decks, and pixel-perfect visuals. But what truly defines your brand is behavior.

Do you follow through? Do you keep promises? Do you do the right thing when it's hard? Do your actions align with your stated values?

People might forget your positioning statement. But they will remember if you owned your mistake, whether your returns process was human, and if your policies treated them like they mattered.

A customer might not describe your brand with brand language, but they can share how it made them feel. That's the true brand memory. And that's what they'll talk about.

Airbnb:
A Brand That Goes Beyond the App

Airbnb is a prime example of a brand that extends well beyond its platform. The brand isn't just the logo or the interface—it's the feeling of checking into a home in an unfamiliar city and feeling like you belong.

It's the host's helpfulness. The tone of the pre-arrival messages. The cleanliness of the space. The feeling of comfort—or discomfort—that lingers with you long after checkout.

Airbnb's official slogan may be "Belong Anywhere," but the true reflection of the brand is in whether that promise is kept or broken.

And in this way, the brand is present in living rooms, kitchens, and neighborhoods around the world. It is built by thousands of hosts and guests every day. That's not something marketing can control, but it's something the company must continually support.

Living the Brand from Within

If your employees don't understand your brand, your customers won't either.

Your internal team should be able to explain what your brand represents—and how that appears in everyday actions. This isn't just about memorizing values; it's about embodying them.

When teams are aligned, the brand feels natural. Decision-making speeds up. Messaging stays consistent. Trust is established. Momentum increases.

When teams are misaligned, the brand becomes fractured. People pull in different directions. Customers receive mixed messages. And belief starts to fade.

That's why internal alignment isn't just a human resources priority—it's a company-wide priority.

The Brand Doesn't Belong to You

In the end, no matter how much strategy you develop, how well you write, or how beautifully you design, your brand isn't truly yours.

It belongs to those who experience it.

It belongs to the customers who express their feelings to others. The employees who bring it into meetings. The community who engages with it in public spaces. The partners who choose whether to support it. The advocates who defend it. And the critics who question it.

Your job isn't to control every impression. It's to earn consistency, build trust, and act with clarity—so that wherever your brand appears, it feels just like you.

The Heart of the Matter

- **If a stranger encountered your brand for the first time—anywhere—would they understand your message?**
- **Every touchpoint tells a story. Ensure yours conveys the right one.**
- **Don't just define your brand. Live it, because your brand already exists—whether you show up for it or not.**

Chapter 14
Consistency Wins
Steadiness Builds Confidence

PEOPLE DON'T FALL IN love with brands in just one moment. They fall in love gradually—through consistency.

Inconsistent brands might grab attention. But consistent brands gain trust. They create familiarity, reliability, and comfort. And those are the building blocks of loyalty.

You don't need to be flashy. You don't have to reinvent yourself every quarter. But you do need to show up consistently—the same way across every channel, every product, every experience.

Because in branding, consistency isn't boring. It's magnetic.

Why Consistency Matters

Branding is a relationship, and like any relationship, it needs trust to grow.

If a friend changes personalities every time you see them (hyper one day, quiet the next, then dismissive) you don't feel safe with them. You don't know what to expect, and eventually, you drift away.

The same is true for brands.

If your tone on social media is casual but your in-store experience feels cold and corporate, the customer senses that dissonance, even if they can't quite express it. If your packaging claims to be eco-friendly but your shipping materials are wasteful, trust begins to decline. If your ads promote warmth and inclusion but your customer service feels robotic or indifferent, the magic is broken.

Consistency isn't about rigidity—it's about coherence. It's how you earn belief.

Familiarity Builds Trust

People go back to what feels familiar. Familiarity is comforting, and comfort makes you seem less risky to choose again.

That's why your favorite brands don't surprise you—they reassure you. They make you feel like "I know what I'm going to get. I trust this experience."

And when someone reaches that level of comfort, they don't shop around. They don't need to. They've already chosen you—and your consistency continues to earn that loyalty.

Great Brands Make One Promise—and Keep It

At the core of consistency is a promise. The top brands don't make numerous claims. They make a single, clear, compelling promise—then they follow through on it every time.

- FedEx promises overnight delivery, and it delivers.
- Chick-fil-A promises politeness and quick service, and it trains every employee to deliver that experience.
- Trader Joe's promises unique quality with friendly staff, and it consistently delivers on that promise in every store, every week.

These brands don't succeed because they're the cheapest or most fashionable. They succeed because they're reliably consistent in the best way.

You know what to expect—and that expectation is always met or surpassed.

That's the essence of brand equity: consistent satisfaction.

Consistency Doesn't Mean Sameness

Being consistent doesn't mean dull. It means being recognizable—even as you evolve.

The best brands constantly evolve. They update their packaging, refresh their tone, and launch new products. But even with these changes, one thing remains the same: A thread runs through everything they do.

That's because consistency isn't about duplication. It's about alignment. A new ad campaign might look different, but it still feels like the brand. A new feature might surprise you, but it fits the brand's story. A new social post might go viral, but it's still on-brand in tone and spirit.

Consistency isn't about repeating yourself—it's about reinforcing yourself.

Costco: Steady Conviction

Costco exemplifies brand consistency. Their products may change and their seasonal displays may evolve, but their core mission stays the same: delivering value and building trust with members.

From the membership model to the decision to cap markups at a fixed margin, everything they do reflects the same brand conviction.

That's why members stay loyal for decades—because Costco doesn't need to remind you who they are. They prove it—consistently.

Consistency Enhances Memory

A consistent brand isn't just trustworthy—it's memorable.

Think of a jingle you can't forget, a logo you recognize instantly, or a scent that evokes a store experience. These things stick because of repetition.

Repetition builds recognition. Recognition fosters recall. And recall results in preference.

If your brand constantly changes its look, tone, message, or values, you're not building recognition. You're creating confusion. And confused people don't commit.

Brand consistency is the key to becoming someone's first choice. Not because you're louder but because you're clear.

When Consistency Fails

We've all seen brands chase trends—suddenly shifting their tone to sound younger, launching quirky campaigns out of nowhere, or redesigning their logo to the point of stripping away their identity.

Sometimes these stunts attract attention. But they often confuse core customers and weaken hard-earned brand equity.

A single misaligned move—a tone-deaf ad, a gimmicky activation, or a messy rebrand—can cause friction that's hard to resolve. The customer then starts to wonder, "Wait, who are they now?"

And once your brand's identity is questioned, belief in it becomes fragile.

That's why great brands don't chase trends—they pursue truth. Their truth.

Consistency Doesn't Occur by Chance

You can't assume consistency will develop naturally. It must be intentionally built into every part of the organization.

That means:

- Clear brand guidelines that cover more than just fonts and colors
- Onboarding that teaches tone, storytelling, and voice
- Aligning internal values, messaging, and behavior
- Leadership modeling the brand through their speech and actions
- Empowering teams to ask, "Is this on-brand?"

Consistency is everyone's responsibility—from the CEO to the copywriter to the person answering the phones.

When everyone has ownership of the brand, consistency becomes the norm.

The Reward Is Emotional, Not Just Functional

Superficially, consistency seems like a branding tactic. But the real reward is emotional.

Consistency fosters safety. It creates a sense of "I know them." And in a chaotic, unpredictable world, that kind of emotional safety is priceless.

Customers don't just want to be satisfied. They want to feel secure.

When your brand becomes a place customers trust to come back to—reliably, comfortably, confidently—you've built more than loyalty.

You have established trust in a chaotic world.

The Heart of the Matter

- Consistency isn't just about repeating a message; it's about reinforcing your identity.
- When customers know what to expect and you deliver, you earn more than just business. You earn trust.
- In a distracted world, consistency stands out as the signal. Everything else is just noise.

Chapter 15
Clarify Your Message
Clear Beats Clever

IN A NOISY, FAST-PACED world, brands often think that being clever or complex makes them appear sophisticated. The reality is the opposite: Clarity is the foundation of trust.

When people struggle to understand what you do, why you matter, or how to connect with you, they rarely take the time to figure it out. They move on.

Confusion causes friction. Friction pushes people away.

Clarity is more than just a communication skill; it gives you a competitive advantage.

Why Clarity Wins

A clear brand makes people feel smart for understanding it—not foolish for missing the point. Clarity makes decisions easier, reduces anxiety, and quickly builds confidence. When someone knows exactly what you stand for and what you offer, they relax and are drawn in.

Complex messaging and clever slogans may catch fleeting attention, but clarity builds lasting trust. And trust—not just awareness—is what keeps brands alive over time.

The Cost of Complexity

Complexity exists in many areas. It's in overloaded websites filled with options and jargon that are hard to navigate. It's in marketing copy full of buzzwords only insiders understand. It appears in inconsistent language across channels, making people question if it's even the same company. It also includes products or services that need lengthy explanations before consumers understand what they do or are.

For every extra mental step that customers take, you risk losing them. Complexity feels like uncertainty. If you can't explain what you do simply, people question whether you truly understand your offering—or worse, if you're hiding something.

Clarity vs. Cleverness

Inside organizations, cleverness often receives praise. Teams celebrate witty headlines, inside jokes, or bold campaigns. But customers aren't inside your building. They lack the context needed to understand hidden meanings.

Clarity, on the other hand, feels good to customers. It respects their time and attention. It allows them to understand your message immediately. Cleverness might spark curiosity, but clarity builds confidence. And confidence is what drives people to act.

The Four Dimensions of Clarity

Clarity isn't just about word choice; it should influence every aspect of your brand experience. Four dimensions determine whether people truly "get" you.

1. Message Clarity

Your words should address three questions:

- What do you do?
- Who do you do it for?
- Why does it matter?

And they should do so clearly. If someone can't explain your value in one sentence after visiting your site or hearing your pitch, you're unclear.

2. Visual Clarity

Design conveys meaning as effectively as text. Visual clutter, inconsistent typography, and mismatched imagery confuse customers before they even read your message. Clean, focused design minimizes mental effort and enhances understanding.

3. Process Clarity

What happens after someone says "Yes"? When sign-up procedures, onboarding steps, or purchase processes feel complicated, clarity vanishes. Smooth, intuitive systems reassure people they've made the right choice.

4. Decision Clarity

Great brands help customers make decisions quickly. They eliminate irrelevant choices, guide people to the best fit, and make trade-offs easy to understand.

When these four dimensions align, your brand feels clear, honest, and reliable.

Stages of Clarity

Clarity develops gradually in stages, like trust or culture.

Stage 1: Confused Branding

Messaging is inconsistent. Different teams describe the brand in varying ways. Materials are produced for internal approval rather than to promote clear external understanding.

Stage 2: Working Toward Defining the Brand

The company can articulate a basic value proposition, but inconsistencies still exist. Marketing, product, and customer experience are not fully aligned.

Stage 3: The Brand's Becoming Clearer

Language becomes sharper, design feels more cohesive, processes are easier to navigate, and employees describe the brand clearly and consistently. Customers repeat the message—a sign it's resonating.

Stage 4: Clarity Becomes Instinctive

Clarity becomes second nature. Employees and customers don't have to think about what you do or why it matters—it's obvious. At this stage, your brand no longer struggles to attract attention because it has already earned it.

Zoom: A Brand Built on Clarity

Few contemporary brands demonstrate clarity quite like Zoom.

When Zoom launched, the video conferencing market was already filled with established players—Webex, Skype, GoToMeeting. Yet Zoom quickly gained ground because of a simple promise: "Video communication that just works."

Zoom didn't try to sound clever. It didn't overwhelm users with features or complicated pricing tiers. It focused on making virtual communication seamless.

Joining a meeting was a simple experience: Users only needed a link. No downloads, no complicated setup.

The interface was as clean as possible with minimal buttons, intuitive controls, and a distraction-free design.

They delivered consistent messaging: From the website to product tutorials, Zoom communicated in clear language anyone could understand.

They became known for dependability, and the technology reinforced the brand message—fast connections, clear audio, smooth video.

During the pandemic, as the world suddenly moved online, Zoom became a lifeline for schools, businesses, and families—not because of aggressive marketing but because its clarity and reliability made it the obvious choice.

Even as competitors hurried to imitate its features, Zoom stayed synonymous with easy communication. The brand made users feel intelligent for choosing it. That confidence fuels long-term loyalty and adoption.

How Leaders Drive Clarity

Clarity isn't just a marketing tactic; it's a leadership responsibility. Leaders either sharpen the message or add to the confusion. The most effective and successful brands demonstrate a clear sense of purpose and meaning to the consumer. That clarity starts at the top and flows through the entire organization.

It's guided by leaders who:

- **Make decisions.** Indecision leads to complexity. A leader who clearly defines priorities provides teams with focus to craft simple, coherent messages.

- **Simplify the strategy.** If executives can't explain the vision clearly, their teams won't be able to communicate it effectively.
- **Eliminate internal clutter.** Overlapping initiatives, mixed signals, and contradictory directives first confuse employees—then customers.
- **Value simplicity.** When organizations praise complexity—more slides, more features, more talking—clarity suffers. Leaders should emphasize focus and directness.

Clarity isn't about doing less. It's about making intentional choices and communicating them clearly.

Clarity Builds Trust

Every brand makes promises. But you need clarity if you want those promises to seem believable.

When customers clearly understand what you represent, what you provide, and what you won't compromise on, they feel confident choosing you. Transparency depends on clarity. And trust depends on transparency.

Confusing brands create doubt. Clear brands build trust.

From Clarity to Connection

Clarity not only makes understanding easier but also strengthens emotional bonds. People favor brands that simplify life. They keep coming back to brands that reduce stress, cut down effort, and remove uncertainty.

When your message is clear, there's no need to shout. Customers lean in because they feel at ease. Comfort builds trust. Trust encourages loyalty.

Clarity also enhances creativity. When you know exactly who you are and what you stand for, you can tell stories more confidently and design experiences more effectively. Simplicity doesn't weaken emotion—it strengthens it.

The brands people talk about aren't just recognizable—they're easy to understand and remember. They give customers a reason to share their stories and proudly connect their identity to the brand. That kind of support must be earned through clarity and honesty.

The Heart of the Matter

- **Can you describe your brand in one sentence?**
- **Complexity hides meaning; clarity shows it.**
- **When people immediately understand and trust you, they don't just see your brand—they believe in it.**

Chapter 16
Be Brag-Worthy
Loyal Customers Love to Share

IN AN ERA WHERE every purchase is scrutinized, every moment can be shared on social media, and every experience could go viral—whether good or bad—your brand is influenced not only by what you say about it but also by what others are eager to say on your behalf.

And the ultimate victory? When people don't just recommend your brand…they brag about it. That's emotional gold.

You've seen it happen—around dinner tables, in group chats, on Instagram stories. Someone can't wait to tell friends about a product they've discovered. They aren't being paid or prompted. They take pride in being the first in their circle to share something meaningful.

That kind of excitement creates a gravitational pull no traditional campaign can match. It's genuine advocacy—and when your brand ignites it, growth ceases to be pushed and begins to be pulled.

From Utility to Identity

We no longer just buy products; we buy brands that become part of who we are.

This shift from utility to identity doesn't happen by accident. It is intentionally created through design, storytelling, and experiences that resonate deeply. Some brands go beyond just functioning to become personal symbols. People proudly take them to meetings, share them online, and mention them in conversations—not to brag but to show their strong connection to the brand.

When a brand fosters that level of connection, advocacy spreads naturally. The results are more effective than any paid effort.

Wearing Rhone—a men's activewear brand known for premium fabrics and tailored design—isn't just about comfort; it represents a lifestyle. Driving a Tesla isn't only about getting from point A to point B; it also signifies a belief in innovation and sustainability. Choosing a small local boutique over a large retailer tells a story about supporting community and authenticity.

When your brand becomes a part of someone's self-expression, you don't need to ask them to share. They want to.

The Psychology of Bragging

Psychologists refer to this phenomenon as "social proof." We are influenced by seeing others—especially those we respect—choose a brand. Advocacy at this level doesn't seem like marketing; it feels like belonging.

When someone brags about a brand, they're not just recommending it—they're affirming their own taste, identity, and values. It's not about ego; it's about connection.

Brands that understand this don't manipulate people into talking. They create genuine moments that make customers feel proud to say, "This feels like me."

Make It Easy to Share, Not Just Easy to Buy

Brag-worthy brands go beyond just offering great products. They craft shareable experiences—small moments that make customers feel special enough to spread the word.

It's a handwritten thank you note tucked into a package, a personal follow-up message after resolving an issue, or a surprise upgrade or gift that feels unexpected and personal.

These gestures don't just satisfy customers—they delight them. People can't believe a brand noticed, cared, and acted in such a human way. Stories like these spread much more powerfully than advertisements ever could.

Even the way a product is packaged or unboxed can become a conversation starter. Brands that get this don't just prioritize usefulness; they prioritize shareability—making every touchpoint something customers want to talk about.

Oura Ring: Making Wellness a Status Symbol

Few brands exemplify brag-worthy advocacy better than the Oura Ring, the sleek wearable that monitors sleep, activity, and overall health.

From the outside, it looks like minimalist jewelry. But for those who wear it, it's much more than an accessory. It supports personal well-being. It's also a statement about lifestyle and self-awareness.

From a design perspective, Oura doesn't resemble typical tech gadgets. It appears more like high-end fashion, making it easier and more attractive for people to showcase.

Oura's message isn't about steps or calories—it's about holistic well-being, elite performance, and better living. That's a story people are proud to share.

Oura wearers—users of the sleek health-tracking device, the Oura Ring—often talk about their daily readiness scores, sharing insights and tips. That community aspect turns personal data into social conversations. High-profile athletes and leaders use Oura, strengthening its reputation as a symbol of personal optimization and discipline.

People who wear Oura rarely just say, "It tracks my sleep." Instead, they tell friends, "This ring changed how I recover and perform." They share screenshots of their health data and discuss how it makes them feel sharper and more balanced.

That's bragging—although not in a boastful way. It's advocacy rooted in real pride in being part of a group working for something better.

Bragging Isn't Bought—It's Built

You don't need complicated referral programs or expensive influencer campaigns to generate brag-worthy advocacy. You need a brand that makes people feel clever for discovering it first, innovative for adopting something ahead of the curve, and recognized for who they are and what they care about.

Give customers language they can use—stories they can share—and you'll build a brand with lasting meaning. Something they can confidently bring into conversations with their friends, family, and colleagues.

Moments Worth Sharing

Some of the most brag-worthy moments happen when brands let customers co-create the experience. It's when sneaker companies offer full customization, then showcase those designs online. Or when LEGO turns fan-built creations into official sets. It's also when food and beverage start-ups encourage playful, shareable rituals around their products.

When people feel like they've contributed to creating something—whether it's customizing a product or providing feedback that influences it—they're not just talking about what they purchased. They're talking about what they built. That sense of pride fuels organic advocacy that money can't buy.

The Leadership Question

Leaders can spark brag-worthy moments by asking a simple, often overlooked question in meetings:

"What can we do this week that makes someone so proud they can't help but tell a friend?"

It's a completely different mindset from chasing clicks or impressions. Instead of asking how to reach more people, you focus on making one person feel truly connected—and confident enough to share that feeling with others. From one to hundreds to thousands, it will spread if you do it right.

That's how bragging starts: one story, one proud customer at a time.

From Pride to Belief

When people brag about your brand, they're not just spreading awareness—they're demonstrating belief. They show that your values, design, and behavior resonate so strongly that they want to make it part of their identity.

When your brand inspires that level of pride, you go beyond just being talked about. You become celebrated. And celebration has lasting power.

But pride alone won't sustain connection forever. To turn temporary bragging into lifelong advocacy, brands must go farther—crafting experiences that evoke not just pride but genuine human emotion, the kind that endures long after trends fade.

The Heart of the Matter

- **Advocacy can't be bought—it develops when customers feel proud to associate with your brand.**
- **Create brag-worthy moments for customers—something so personal and memorable that they can't resist sharing it.**
- **When people boast about your brand, your message ceases to be marketing and becomes part of their story. That's when you stop seeking attention and begin earning belief.**

Chapter 17
Design for Emotion–Not Just for Attention

IN TODAY'S WORLD OF endless feeds, fast swipes, and constant noise, the brands that truly stand out aren't the loudest. They're the ones that evoke genuine feelings. They don't just chase clicks; they create meaningful moments—ones people remember, talk about, and return to.

Designing for emotion isn't just about looks. It's about shaping how people feel through every interaction—before, during, and after they connect with your brand. Because emotions don't just capture a moment—they form memories, and those memories influence what happens next: affinity, loyalty, and advocacy.

Why Emotion Matters More than Ever

We live in a fast-paced, high-choice, low-trust culture. People have more options than ever before, but their attention and trust are declining. In this environment, features and benefits don't make you memorable—feelings do.

Consider why people share unboxing videos. It's not just about revealing what's inside a package; it's the excitement, joy, and surprise that make it worth sharing.

Or consider why dog owners post photos of their BarkBox deliveries. It's not just the toys—it's the joy of seeing their dog excited, the emotional moment that's worth capturing and sharing.

These moments serve as emotional touchpoints. Each one is an opportunity for your brand to build a memory, not just to deliver a product. And memories have much greater staying power than messages.

Emotion fuels habits. Habits, over time, shape brand value.

Beyond Utility: Telling an Emotional Story

Great design isn't only about looking good or working well. It's about telling a story that people feel part of.

Every image, word, sound, and sequence in your brand experience should help tell your story.

Take Figma. On paper, it's just a collaboration tool. But through thoughtful design, it empowers teams, encourages alignment, and sparks creativity. It reduces friction and boosts confidence. The emotion isn't just productivity—it's pride in working together more effectively.

Consider Aesop. It's soap, yes—but everything about it is designed to feel like more. The minimalist amber bottles with their clean labels look stylish. The botanical scents and textures turn handwashing into a sensory ritual. And the stores themselves, often designed like art galleries, make even the act of shopping feel intentional and elevated. Aesop shows that a simple product can be transformed into an experience people want to feel again and again.

Disney: A Master Class in Emotional Design

No brand has mastered emotional design quite like Disney.

Disney doesn't just build theme parks or make movies. It designs moments of wonder that live forever in people's memories.

At the parks, it's about creating seamless stories. From the first ticket purchase to the last ride, every touchpoint feels like part of the same narrative. It feels magical.

The focus on multi-sensory experiences—including the music, lighting, scents, and tactile design—combines to create immersive worlds. A child doesn't just see Cinderella's castle—they feel awe and excitement just walking toward it.

The Disney "cast members" are trained to create spontaneous emotional moments—whether it's kneeling to talk to a shy child or staying totally in character when a family meets their favorite Disney icon.

Disney intentionally crafts moments of surprise—hidden Mickeys, unexpected character encounters, behind-the-scenes glimpses—fostering emotions people cherish long after they leave.

After visiting any Disney park worldwide, guests don't just remember what they saw. They recall how they felt—enchanted, joyful, safe, inspired. That emotional memory is why Disney remains one of the most beloved family brands in the world.

Some might say you can enjoy great rides at other theme parks or love family movies made by other studios, but you can't easily replicate Disney's emotional design. That feeling belongs to Disney because it's been intentionally crafted, touchpoint by touchpoint, for decades.

Designing Every Touchpoint to Evoke Emotion

You don't need Disney's scale or budget to create emotionally impactful experiences.

Every small moment—especially the overlooked ones—can serve as a powerful emotional connection. It can be reflected in the tone of your error messages, whether harsh or comforting. The language in your confirmation emails can be perfunctory or warm and appreciative. Even the way a customer service rep signs off a call—with thanks and personality, and hopefully not with "Please stay on the line for a survey"—can create a connection.

These aren't just operational details; they are chances to show care, evoke joy, and build pride. Successful brands recognize that seemingly small details often leave the most lasting emotional impact.

Consistency of Feeling

We've talked about the impact and importance of consistency, but it's essential to remember that it's not just about visual design or messaging—it's also about emotional alignment.

Consistent emotions build trust. When every interaction feels the same emotionally, people relax because they know what to expect. That sense of comfort is part of why they keep coming back.

Emotion Without Manipulation

Designing for emotion doesn't mean tugging at heartstrings. It's not about creating artificial drama or forced sentimentality.

It's about genuine connection: making someone smile when they expected indifference. Making them feel understood when they often feel ignored. Giving them a sense of belonging when they usually feel anonymous.

When you do this, emotion turns into a genuine part of your brand—not just a tactic.

Ask Better Emotional Questions

Emotion is seldom accidental. To intentionally shape it, you need to ask questions that extend beyond the functional.

To better understand your customers and their connection with your brand, consider questions like: What do we want people to feel when they first encounter our brand? What emotions should linger after they walk away? Are we creating memorable moments? Do our emotional cues feel authentic and consistent wherever someone encounters us?

Understanding the answers to these and similar questions influences design choices in ways that no style guide can fully cover. It moves you beyond "Does this look good?" to "Does this make someone feel good?"

From Emotion to Lasting Connection

Designing for emotion not only captures attention but also builds loyalty. People don't stick with brands because of a single campaign; they stay because the brand consistently makes them feel something meaningful.

When you design for emotion, you forge a connection that competitors with similar products or services cannot duplicate. They can match your prices or features, but they can't copy the feeling of trust, joy, or wonder you've intentionally created.

The strongest emotional bonds form when customers aren't just touched by your brand—they feel like they are part of it. When you invite them to co-create experiences, you move from merely delivering emotions to sharing ownership. That's when customers change from buyers into believers. And that's where we're headed next—exploring how co-creation can turn connection into a real community.

The Heart of the Matter

- **Attention can be bought; emotion must be earned.**
- **Attention diminishes rapidly; emotional resonance makes a lasting impact.**

Chapter 18
Customers as Creators
Listen to Their Cues

THE MOST INFLUENTIAL BRANDS today aren't just followed—they're co-created.

In an era when people want to be more than passive consumers, leading brands are evolving into platforms for engagement. They're no longer based on one-way communication or top-down campaigns. Instead, they encourage participation. They open doors for customers to do more than just buy—they enable customers to help shape the brand itself.

When this happens, the relationship moves from being purely transactional to something more personal, emotional, and enduring.

Imagine this: A customer submits a product idea through an open platform, and months later, that idea turns into a real product—launched, celebrated, and bearing their name on the packaging. That person would likely go from casual buyer to lifelong advocate—not because of a discount or loyalty perk but because they became part of the brand's DNA.

That's the power of turning customers into creators.

Consumer Participation Is a Key Goal

Once upon a time, brands controlled the entire story. They crafted the message, refined it for the media, and delivered it to the market. Consumers either accepted or rejected it. We discussed this earlier when talking about how brands no longer own the full conversation. Here, we'll go deeper because participation isn't just a change in storytelling; it has become the main goal for building belief.

Today, the most successful brands will share the story.

LEGO recognized this early with LEGO Ideas, a platform where fans submit ideas for new sets. Other fans vote. Winning ideas are turned into products, with the original fan credited on the box. That's not just customer feedback—it's a creative partnership.

Converse followed a similar philosophy by allowing fans to personalize sneakers and submit designs for campaigns. The product itself becomes a canvas, turning the customer into a visible co-creator.

Even niche brands can succeed with this approach.

Ooni Pizza Ovens started as a backyard innovation. It grew by cultivating a global community of pizza lovers who didn't just use Ooni's products—they created recipes, made how-to videos, and redefined outdoor cooking. On Instagram, fans often share their own pizza creations and exchange tips on dough and toppings. On YouTube, some of the most viewed Ooni tutorials aren't made by the brand at all—they come from passionate customers. Ooni embraced this, amplifying user-generated content and even collaborating with fans to produce official recipe books. By embracing that energy instead of trying to control it, Ooni built a culture where customers became collaborators and ambassadors.

When people become this committed, pride takes over. They stop talking about what they bought and start sharing who they've become through your brand.

User-Generated Content vs. User-Generated Branding

Marketers have long talked about user-generated content (UGC)—photos, reviews, social posts. That's valuable, but it's only the beginning.

The true power lies in user-generated branding (UGB). This is when people aren't just making content about your brand—they're shaping its identity.

Think of fans who become deeply engaged with your brand. They talk to their friends or create new connections on chat forums, all because of their passion for your brand. These aren't just unauthorized distractions—they're signs your brand has achieved emotional and cultural significance.

Executives often feel uneasy about this, fearing they might lose control. However, the most innovative brands take the opposite approach. They view UGB as a source of energy, not a threat. They trust their community enough to let it influence tone, language, and campaign ideas. That trust deepens connections and creates an authenticity that no top-down marketing can match.

Take Duolingo as an example. Its playful green owl mascot became a viral sensation on TikTok—not because it was planned but because users started making jokes about its obsessive notifications. Instead of ignoring it, Duolingo leaned into it—the brand posted videos of the mascot "stalking" people in offices, crashing Zoom calls, and even guilt-tripping users for skipping lessons. By responding in character and amplifying the humor, Duolingo turned what could have been a complaint into a cultural wink and nod. The result? Affection, virality, and a boost in loyalty built on shared creativity.

Focus on Input, Not Only Output

Many brands concentrate too heavily on perfecting what they share externally: the message, visuals, and campaign. However, the most engaging brands are built for conversation, not just a monologue.

Notion, the productivity app, thrives because it allows users to create and share templates, fundamentally influencing the product's development.

Twitch, the streaming platform, constantly evolves based on feedback from its streamers and viewers. It's not a static product—it's a dynamic, collaboratively shaped experience.

Even legacy brands can embrace this shift. Mattel's Barbie, once seen as rigid and outdated, has regained cultural relevance by embracing fan-driven reinterpretations. Whether it's customizable avatars or campaigns that highlight playful fan stories, Mattel stopped trying to control Barbie's meaning and started collaborating with the people who loved (and sometimes critiqued) her.

Opening up doesn't mean losing your values. Think of it like hosting a dinner party—you set the menu, the music, the tone. But the real magic of the evening comes from the guests—their stories and laughter and the connections they make.

Brands that clearly articulate their principles while fostering creativity promote safe, vibrant environments for collaboration.

Co-Creation Shapes Culture

When people engage with your brand creatively, they aren't just interacting with you—they're building connections with one another.

That connection drives culture. Fans build communities that not only support your brand but also help it grow and defend it. Often, they do this more genuinely—and more effectively—than your own marketing team ever could.

Imagine a small fashion brand that invites customers to design patches for limited-edition jackets. Thousands of fans submit their designs, and some are produced. Years later, those jackets become collectibles, telling a story that belongs to both the brand and the community. That's cultural co-creation—something no ad campaign could replicate.

This idea isn't new to me. Years ago, when I worked at Toys "R" Us, I imagined creating what I called a "Kid's Panel." A group of curious, outspoken kids would regularly come in to test toys before their launch. We wouldn't ask leading questions or filter their feedback—we'd simply observe them playing.

In an unfiltered environment like that, we could see which toys sparked excitement and imagination, which ones held attention longer than a few minutes, and which ones were discarded and forgotten almost instantly.

It wasn't pure co-creation, but it was authentic insight from the people who matter most: the end users.

If we had fully implemented that idea, it would have altered our product strategy—not because we had gathered more data but because we had involved kids in shaping the experience.

That lesson has stayed with me: Brands are always more powerful when they include customers—not just researchers or executives—in the conversation.

From Participation to Proof

Co-creation is powerful because it encourages emotional investment. People care more about things they've helped create.

But co-creation also involves responsibility. When someone contributes to your brand—through ideas, creativity, or advocacy—they're placing their trust in you. They believe that their input matters and you'll respect it.

That belief must be validated daily. If you ask for input, you need to acknowledge it and act on it, or at least explain why you didn't. If you invite customers to collaborate, ensure they know you have considered and value their input. To build a community, you must nurture and protect it, not exploit it.

Advocacy, creativity, and participation mean little if a brand doesn't consistently demonstrate they're worthy of that trust. Proof isn't a one-time event or a campaign—it's a continuous practice. And it's how lasting belief is built.

The Heart of the Matter

- Challenge yourself and your team to find out how customers can influence the story.
- When you make room for co-creation, you do more than just build community—you start to nurture trust.
- Show people through everything you do that their trust has been earned.

Chapter 19
Prove It Daily
Trust Is Built Every Day

TALK IS CHEAP.

Especially when it comes to branding.

You can say you're customer-first, purpose-driven, or the most innovative player in your space. But those claims mean nothing if they aren't supported by action.

In today's world—where reviews spread faster than ads and every promise is met with suspicion—brands aren't judged by what they say. They're judged by what they prove.

And you can't do it just once. You have to prove yourself every day.

The Burden of Proof

Every brand makes promises. That's simple.

The hard part is consistently keeping those promises—not just once but every time. Every purchase, interaction, scroll, and conversation is an opportunity to prove your value—or to fall short.

And here's the thing: People are paying attention. Not just your customers but also your employees, partners, investors, and community.

They're not just paying attention to your mission statement. They're watching how you behave.

- Do your actions align with your words?
- Do your products deliver what they promise?
- Do you treat people the way your values suggest?

If the answer is yes—and it's consistently yes—you build trust. If not, you lose something much more valuable than sales: credibility.

Proving It Isn't Just a Campaign

Proof isn't in your brand campaign; it's in your operational discipline. You showcase it in:

- The way your service team responds under pressure
- The durability of your product six months after purchase
- The look of your store on a slow Monday afternoon
- The way your service team follows up after a complaint
- The feeling someone has after leaving your website—did it work, did it help, did it respect their time?

Proof is tangible, emotional, and authentic—and it's measured one moment at a time.

Trust Is Built in the Small Things

Most people don't remember the brand promise from your website. But they remember that:

- You responded to their message within minutes

when they had a problem.
- Their order arrived exactly when you said it would.
- A human—not a script—talked to them on the phone.
- Your packaging seemed thoughtful.
- The product worked perfectly, exactly as described.

Small things aren't insignificant; they're signals. Repeating them helps build trust.

One missed expectation might be forgiven. But repeated inconsistency? That erodes belief.

Actions over Intentions

Many brands have good intentions. They truly want to do the right thing. But intention without follow-through can be worse than saying nothing.

Don't claim to care about sustainability unless you've addressed your supply chain. Don't say you're committed to inclusion unless it's evident in your leadership, hiring, and content. Don't declare yourself customer-first unless your policies truly reflect empathy.

People aren't seeking perfection. They're seeking alignment—between what you say and what you do.

Brands That Prove It

Certain brands have perfected this skill.

Zappos built its reputation not on shoes but on the obsessive quality of its customer service. Their proof wasn't in slogans—it was in every support interaction, every return, and every delighted customer who received an unexpected upgrade.

Virgin has built its brand on bold experiences and prioritizing customers. From airlines to music to space travel, the proof isn't in ads—it's in how Richard Branson's companies challenge norms, impress customers, and stand out with personality.

Red Bull isn't just about selling an energy drink. It backs up its brand by supporting extreme sports, organizing record-breaking stunts, and cultivating a culture of adrenaline that matches its promise. Customers don't need to wonder what Red Bull stands for—they see it in action.

These brands couldn't be more different—shoes, airlines, and energy drinks—yet they share a common principle: They demonstrate who they are through consistent actions, not empty words.

You Can't Out-Market Inconsistency

No amount of creative brilliance can fix a damaged experience.

You can't pay your way out of poor service. You can't market your way past a misleading product. You can't story-tell your way around hypocrisy.

If you overpromise and underdeliver, eventually the gap catches up with you—and people walk away.

Marketing amplifies. It doesn't hide.

If the truth underneath isn't solid, all you're doing is exposing the cracks.

Proving It Fosters the Right Kind of Growth

When a brand consistently demonstrates its value day after day, growth happens naturally.

- Customers return without needing to be chased.
- Word of mouth has a greater impact than paid media.

- Loyalty isn't only about discounts—it's about trust.
- Teams feel proud rather than just pressured.

You don't have to shout as loudly when people already believe you. That's a quieter, more sustainable form of power.

The Role of Leadership

Proving it begins at the top.

Leaders set the tone for whether brand values are merely words—or guiding principles. They shape the culture of accountability, ownership, and daily follow-through.

A leader who demonstrates integrity creates a company that proves its value. A leader who neglects the brand between marketing cycles fosters confusion and mistrust.

The best leaders understand that you don't prove it just once a year. You prove it every single day through every decision, hire, policy, and compromise not made.

The Ultimate Proof?
When People Don't Doubt

You'll know your brand is succeeding when people no longer need convincing.

- When customers skip comparison shopping and go straight to you.
- When employees advocate for your culture without being asked.
- When press coverage and community sentiment reflect what you've said all along.

In that world, trust turns into momentum. And momentum turns into belief. Not because you launched a brilliant campaign but because people kept experiencing your truth—again and again and again.

The Heart of the Matter

- **Talk is exposure. Proof is ownership.**
- **People don't trust what you say. They trust what you show.**
- **Branding isn't just about saying it properly. It's about living it authentically—every single day.**

Chapter 20
Enhance Personalization
People Want to Feel Seen

PEOPLE DON'T ONLY WANT to be served—they want to be acknowledged.

Every time someone interacts with a brand, they subconsciously wonder: "Do they know me? Do they understand me? Do they care about what matters to me?"

Personalization is how you respond to those questions. It's how you turn a generic transaction into a meaningful connection. It's how you show that someone isn't just another data point—they're valued, recognized, and remembered.

Personalization Is About More than a Name

Many companies think personalization is just about inserting a first name into an email or sending product suggestions based on previous purchases. These actions only check a box; true personalization goes much further.

Real personalization feels seamless. It predicts needs before customers even ask. It removes obstacles customers once thought they had to face. When executed well, it never feels forced or robotic. Customers don't think, "They personalized this for me." They think, "This brand understands me."

Why Personalization Matters

In today's market, people encounter countless options and decision exhaustion. They don't need more details—they want relevance.

When a brand feels relevant, people naturally come back to it. They stop doubting or comparing because they believe you understand them better than anyone else.

Zara: Fast and Scalable Personalization

Fashion retail is notoriously unpredictable—trends shift overnight, and customer preferences differ by location, climate, and culture. Zara has turned this challenge into its competitive advantage through personalization integrated at every level.

Zara store staff actively gather feedback daily—from items customers try on to requests they can't find. This isn't stored in dashboards; it is sent directly to the merchants that update patterns and inventory weekly.

Unlike many retailers that standardize their offerings worldwide, Zara personalizes collections for each city. The same store layout in New York and Madrid might seem similar, but the products inside reflect local tastes learned through continuous listening.

Zara's app connects to in-store inventory, allowing shoppers to view real-time stock levels and receive recommendations. Online data supports store-level decision-making, blending digital personalization with human observation.

Traditional fashion cycles can last for months. Zara's supply chain is built to transform insights into new clothing in just weeks—demonstrating that personalization isn't just about communication, it's embedded in operations.

This system doesn't promote itself as personalization—it seems like Zara simply "understands" its customers. Shoppers aren't bombarded with endless "We value you" messages. Instead, they walk into stores and consistently find clothing that matches their preferences, sizes, and budget. That's true personalization shown through fabric, not in subject lines.

The Four Levels of Personalization

Personalization grows through four phases:

1. **Recognition:** Identifying customers and recalling their previous purchases so they don't need to repeat information
2. **Relevance:** Customizing offers and messages to fit the customer's current context and needs
3. **Experience Design:** Enhancing navigation, service models, and touchpoints to ensure a seamless journey
4. **Emotional Connection:** Demonstrating shared values, celebrating milestones, and making people genuinely feel understood

When these levels synchronize, personalization no longer seems like marketing and begins to feel like a relationship.

Stages of Personalization

Like trust or culture, personalization evolves through stages.

Stage 1: Basic Interactions

At first, everyone gets the same messages; efficiency takes priority over uniqueness.

Stage 2: Data-Driven Recognition

Basic name recognition and general segmentation is used; it's somewhat personalized but relies on templates.

Stage 3: Contextual Relevance

Needs are anticipated, timing is accurate, and experiences feel almost personalized.

Stage 4: Authentic Personalization

The brand adjusts smoothly; each experience feels one-of-a-kind and naturally tailored to the individual.

Zara operates at higher levels—not just because of advanced AI but because its entire system is designed to listen and respond to real human behavior. A unique blend of human and systemic learning is employed, and customers notice.

The Balance Between Privacy and Empathy

Effective personalization never comes across as invasive. Customers should feel acknowledged, not watched. The top brands understand just enough to simplify lives and enhance experiences, driven by data and empathy.

When personalization borders on manipulation—when recommendations feel too intrusive or private data is used without trust—it can have negative effects. Genuine personalization respects boundaries. It makes people feel safe, not vulnerable.

Leadership's Role

Personalization is more than just a technological feature; it's a leadership choice. Leaders decide whether personalization becomes a key brand strength or an overlooked afterthought. To be effective, leaders must set the right tone and create an environment conducive to success. That means leaders need to:

- **Set goals for personalization:** Decide early that customers will be seen as individuals, not just metrics. Clearly communicate this as a rule, not a choice.
- **Align incentives:** Motivate teams to improve understanding, not just focus on getting clicks or short-term revenue.
- **Break down silos:** Personalization needs a unified view of the customer. Leaders must eliminate barriers that separate data and teamwork.
- **Model empathy:** Technology can offer personalization, but the emphasis should be on encouraging curiosity, learning, and—most important—caring about customer needs to make interactions feel human.

From Personalization to Belief

When personalization works, it does more than just provide convenience—it builds trust. Customers start to think: "This brand understands me, and whether I shop in-store or online, I feel like what I'm offered matches what I'm looking for. My shopping experience is consistently inspiring rather than disappointing. I enjoy the search and never see it as a chore. I feel recognized here."

These beliefs are powerful and enduring. Competitors may imitate your product or match your prices, but they can't easily duplicate the connection you've established with your customers.

Personalization creates an emotional safety net. Even if there's a frustrating delay in shipping or a service hiccup, it feels more understandable and even forgivable because customers feel recognized. It's not just about not being treated as a number; they want to feel like it's all about them. This kind of personalization builds the belief that they've found a brand that feels like home. Like they truly belong.

The Future of Personalization

As technology advances, personalization will become more sophisticated. Still, the winners won't be those that automate the fastest. They'll be the brands that make personalization feel human—blending insight with warmth, efficiency with empathy.

Tomorrow's personalization won't feel like an algorithm at work. It will seem like a trusted guide—quietly anticipating needs, removing obstacles, and making every interaction more meaningful.

Personalization brings you closer to customers, but closeness only matters if it guides them in a meaningful way. A truly powerful brand doesn't just remember your name; it acts as a north star—clear, steady, and unwavering in its beliefs. That's what keeps customers focused when options are plentiful and the path forward seems uncertain.

The Heart of the Matter

- **Are you treating customers like real people or profiles?**
- **Replace generic interactions with genuine moments of recognition.**
- **Proactively show understanding without customers needing to ask.**
- **Showing relevance shows that you care enough to notice.**
- **Transform daily interactions into durable trust.**

Chapter 21
Be the North Star
A Brand People Follow

EVERY SUCCESSFUL BRAND HAS someone—or something—that serves as its north star.

That doesn't mean it has all the answers. It means it offers guidance, especially during the toughest times, to find it.

The north star remains constant regardless of trends. It doesn't follow the news cycle. It doesn't sway with every new, shiny idea.

It's stable, grounding, and constant.

And in today's world of distraction, noise, and complexity, great brands don't just stand for something—they guide everything.

They serve as a compass—both internally and externally—for guiding behavior, setting priorities, and deciding where to go next.

Clarity in a Time of Confusion

Modern business moves quickly. Teams are overwhelmed. Markets are unpredictable. Competitors shift weekly. New technologies appear overnight. AI redefines the playbook by morning.

In this chaos, your brand can serve as a point of stability—not only for customers but also for your team.

When you clearly and confidently define your brand, you provide people with something to latch onto.

That's what a north star does.

It doesn't solve every problem, but it clears up confusion. It helps you say: "This is who we are. This is how we make decisions. This is where we won't compromise."

And when people have that kind of clarity, momentum naturally follows.

Your Brand Should Guide Behavior

Too many companies view the brand as just a message. However, genuine brands function more like operating systems:

- They influence how products are developed.
- They shape how people are hired.
- They determine what gets prioritized.
- They determine how success is evaluated.

That's the true power of a brand with a north star: It doesn't stay on the sidelines; it influences behavior.

When you get it right, the brand goes beyond storytelling: It becomes a basis for decision-making.

And that's where the magic happens.

People Don't Follow Brands; They Follow Conviction

Most people aren't seeking perfection. They're searching for something to believe in.

When your brand has a clear core—a belief system that remains steady through good times and bad—people notice. And they respond.

Customers want to support companies that understand them. Employees prefer to work for leaders who base decisions on values. Partners seek to collaborate with brands that act with integrity, not just ambition.

That's what a north star brand establishes: belief-driven alignment.

You become the brand people rely on to stay honest, even when taking the easier route would be tempting.

When the Brand Leads the Company

In great organizations, the brand leads. It doesn't follow.

- It sets the tone for culture.
- It guides product decisions. It influences growth strategies.
- It determines what not to do, even when numbers tempt otherwise.

It says, "That opportunity might be profitable—but it's not us." Or "That marketing tactic might work for them—but it's not how we show up." Or even "That trend is interesting—but it's not aligned with our promise."

This kind of decision-making only occurs when the brand is fully embedded—not just in marketing decks, but also in the C-suite, on the product roadmap, and in the boardroom.

When that occurs, you're not just seeking relevance. You're leading with purpose.

It's Not Just for the Outside World

Too often, companies view the brand as something you project outward. But the true value of a north star brand becomes apparent internally first.

- It's what helps your teams recognize what good looks like.
- It's what gives people confidence when they're stuck.
- It's what aligns teams that might not otherwise collaborate.

A clear brand direction aligns all departments, even when they face different challenges.

That type of alignment isn't just efficient. It's also powerful. Because when teams move together with shared clarity, the brand becomes stronger with each action.

The Cost of Drifting

Without a north star, teams lose direction. Strategies become unfocused. Priorities become unclear. Cultures become broken.

Suddenly, the sales team is telling one story, the marketing team is pushing another, and the product team is building something that doesn't fit either narrative.

At first, no one notices. Then customers begin to sense the disconnect. Employees start questioning decisions. Brand trust begins to decline.

And once erosion sets in, it's hard to regain belief.

All because no one stopped to ask, "Does this decision align with who we say we are?"

The North Star Isn't Just a Tagline

Your north star isn't just a slogan. It's not a poster on the wall or a mission statement created by committee.

It's your brand's hard-earned truth—the one you fight to protect, the one you return to when everything else gets noisy.

It's what survives when trends fade. It's what your customers would describe even when you're not there. It's what your employees would defend, even if it's not written down.

If you're unsure about your north star, begin by asking:

- What will we never compromise on?
- What are we willing to say no to?
- What would break trust if we made changes?

The answers to those questions are the foundation of your brand's identity.

Leading with the Brand, not Just the Business

The best companies allow their brands to guide their businesses—not the other way around.

That doesn't mean ignoring data or deprioritizing revenue. It means understanding that revenue without resonance is only temporary.

Growth without alignment breeds fragility. But growth driven by a strong, guiding brand? That's enduring. Respected. Trusted.

When your brand is your north star, your company doesn't just grow—it stands for something.

And that's what builds legacy, not just longevity.

The Heart of the Matter

- **A north star brand remains steady, not stagnant. It evolves but never loses direction.**
- **Let your brand lead—not just in marketing but in your decisions.**
- **The more complex the world becomes, the more important clarity is.**

Chapter 22
The Human Touch
Brands That Feel Human Win

WE'RE PRODUCING MORE CONTENT than ever before— and people are disengaging faster than ever.

Why?

Because most of it just sounds like noise. It seems forced, formulaic, or manipulative, like it was made for us, not with us.

And in a world where everyone is posting, publishing, and promoting on a large scale, the brands that stand out aren't the ones producing the most content. They're the ones creating the most human content.

More Doesn't Mean Better

Technology has made it easy to publish endlessly. You can automate posts, batch content for a month in an afternoon, and let AI write your blogs, captions, ads, and emails.

But just because you can doesn't mean you should.

People aren't seeking more content; they want connection. If your brand's content doesn't feel intentional, relatable, or authentic, it won't get noticed— it will be ignored.

Volume without value isn't marketing. It's clutter.

Content Is a Conversation, Not a Broadcast

The best brand content doesn't seem like advertising. It feels like a conversation. It connects with people where they are. It welcomes them. It respects their time and intelligence.

When your content feels human, it builds trust. It gives your audience a reason to care—and come back.

This doesn't mean every post has to be emotional or deep, but it means your content should feel like it comes from a brand made of people, not just pixels.

Human Touch Prevails, Even in an AI World

AI can be useful. It can summarize ideas, assist in brainstorming, and even generate basic content. When used effectively, it can save time and improve efficiency.

But it can't substitute for authenticity.

The brands that will succeed in this new era are the ones that balance automation with intention. They know when to speed up—and when to slow down and make something personal.

Your audience can tell when something was created by someone who understands them…and when it was just produced by a tool.

The signal-to-noise ratio has never been more crucial. And your humanity remains the signal.

Speak the Truth, Not Merely a Tagline

People can sense when content is designed to manipulate, when every sentence is crafted for conversion, and when each line feels like a performance rather than genuine perspective.

Truth cuts through.

You don't need to exaggerate, hype, or over-optimize your message. You just need to mean it.

You don't need a viral stunt; you need a genuine point of view.

You don't need to sound like everyone else; you need to sound like yourself.

That's what content focused on humans looks like.

It represents your brand's heart, not just its KPIs.

Consistency Builds Connection

One great tweet doesn't create a brand. Neither does one slick video. What builds brand trust is a consistent voice, tone, and values over time.

Your content reflects your personality. When people see it across platforms—your website, social media, emails, and packaging—it should all feel like it comes from the same source.

That consistency doesn't occur by chance. It requires discipline. It involves looking beyond campaigns and emphasizing character.

Because ultimately, people don't fall in love with content. They fall in love with brands that feel familiar, trustworthy, and authentic.

Don't Just Follow the Trend— Make It Meaningful

Too many brands chase whatever's trending. They post because it's a holiday. They join the meme of the moment. They copy what competitors are doing.

But relevance without resonance feels superficial.

If you can't add meaning, avoid adding content.

Your brand shouldn't come across as a follower. It should be seen as a voice worth listening to. And that voice should be grounded in your values, not an algorithm.

The question isn't "What's everyone talking about today?" It's "What does our brand genuinely have to say?"

Invite Engagement, Not Just Attention

Great content isn't just something people consume—it's something they respond to.

Ask questions. Share stories. Give behind-the-scenes looks. Spotlight your customers. Let your audience see themselves in what you create.

This isn't about chasing likes or comments. It's about building genuine connection—giving people a reason to engage beyond just scrolling.

Your community doesn't want to feel targeted. They want to feel recognized.

Not All Content Needs to Sell

Not every post requires a call to action. Not every message needs a product plug. Not every email must direct to a checkout page.

Sometimes, the most effective content is the one that simply offers perspective, value, or a moment of delight.

Because when you pause selling for a moment and begin connecting, something shifts.

You go beyond being just a brand in their feed. You become a part of their life.

The Best Content Feels Like It Comes from a Person, Not a Machine

If your content could come from any brand in your category, it's not standing out enough.

Great brand content feels specific. Personal. Rooted in your culture, your language, your humor, and your philosophy.

It seems like someone from your team might have written it—even if it was reviewed, edited, or templated.

It bears your fingerprint. And that's what fosters trust.

In a world where sameness is the norm, personality is what sets us apart.

The Human Advantage

In the rush to expand content and automate communication, don't forget your most powerful tool.

Your humanity. Your quirks. Your voice. Your empathy. Your truth. Your perspective.

That's what your competitors can't imitate. That's what AI can't produce. That's what fosters emotional loyalty.

When you lead with that, your content becomes more than just content. It becomes proof that real people are behind the brand—people worth listening to and trusting.

The Heart of the Matter

- **Human content engages, while automated content only occupies space.**
- **Don't just produce content. Share something genuine.**
- **In a world driven by algorithms, personality is your greatest advantage.**

Chapter 23
Stand Still—Fall Behind
Yesterday Doesn't Guarantee Tomorrow

THERE IS A HARSH reality that every brand ultimately confronts: What brought you here won't take you there.

Even the strongest brands—those with loyal customers, innovative products, and solid reputations—are at risk if they stop evolving. Success breeds comfort. But comfort leads to complacency. And in a marketplace characterized by speed, complexity, and shifting expectations, complacency is risky.

Standing still might seem safe. But it's often the riskiest choice of all.

Because while you're standing still, the world keeps changing around you.

Momentum Wins

Great brands move forward. They learn, adapt, stretch, and evolve. They listen, test, adjust, and improve.

That doesn't mean constant reinvention. It means staying continuously aware. The market shifts. Customers change. Platforms evolve. New competitors appear—not gradually but suddenly.

If you're not constantly assessing your relevance, you're already falling behind.

Momentum isn't just a marketing buzzword. It's a brand's oxygen. It keeps people talking, employees engaged, competitors nervous, and customers leaning in.

When you're moving forward, even just a little, you send a signal: We're still hungry. We're still trying. We're still leading.

And that message is important.

The World Won't Wait

Your customers aren't waiting around for you to catch up. They've already moved on to the next experience that better suits their needs. The next product that understands them more deeply. The next brand that speaks to them like a human and treats them with respect.

They're not paying attention to your timeline. They're focused on their own.

You might think you've secured their loyalty. But what you've really earned is the chance to earn it again and again.

Brands that assume the world will wait for them end up asking, "Where did everyone go?"

Familiarity Isn't the Same as Effectiveness

Comfort is a trap. That same product, that same campaign, and that same email cadence might have worked last year. It might have even worked last month.

But does it still work now? Does it still resonate? Or are you just doing what's always been done?

Your internal team may be fluent in your language and legacy, but your customers don't care about what's familiar to you. They care about what's relevant to them.

Brands don't lose loyal customers all at once. They lose them gradually. Quietly. One ignored update at a time. One underwhelming interaction at a time. One missed opportunity at a time.

The more you coast, the harder it becomes to catch up.

The Cost of Inaction

Many brands don't fail because of one bad decision. They fail because they don't make decisions. They stall. They wait. They default to "next quarter."

And in the meantime:

- New players join the scene.
- Customers seek alternatives.
- Your message begins to sound outdated.
- Your story gets lost in the noise.

You become a brand defined by what you used to be.

And eventually, the most troubling question emerges: "Do people still care?"

Change Doesn't Have to Be Big, But It Needs to Be Genuine

Not every update has to be a revolution. In fact, the most effective brand evolution often appears subtle from the outside.

But what really matters is the intention behind it.

- Match your tone to how your audience speaks now.
- Refresh your creativity without losing your core.
- Enhance your experience to reduce friction.
- Broaden your understanding of whom you serve and how.

Small changes send a strong message: We're paying attention.

And attention—when earned consistently—is the foundation of belief.

Leadership Sets the Pace

A company can only progress as quickly as its leadership permits.

If your C-suite focuses more on protecting yesterday's playbook than exploring what's next, movement slows down. If teams are rewarded for consistency instead of curiosity, progress stalls. If culture punishes experimentation, you'll never try what might actually work.

Great brand leaders understand the difference between discipline and rigidity. They know how to safeguard what's important while nurturing what's ready to develop. They recognize that not changing is also a risk.

A leader who's too afraid to try new things is often the first to be replaced when the business begins to fall behind.

Legacy Is Not a Strategy

A strong history doesn't ensure a successful future.

Legacy can be a powerful asset—but only if it's alive. Only if you're still contributing to it. Only if you're actively earning the right to be remembered.

Some brands cling to the past as if it will save them. But history doesn't create relevance. Relevance comes from being in the present, responding to what matters now, and moving forward with purpose.

Otherwise, you're only a memory, and memories don't fuel growth.

The Disruptors Are Already Here

The category disruptors aren't coming. They've already arrived. They lack your history. They lack your scale. But they have speed. They have simplicity. And they can connect in ways that feel more immediate and personal.

They don't seek permission. They disregard the old rules. They act quickly and aren't waiting for you to catch up.

If you're still discussing whether to test an idea they already launched last month, you're not in the same race. You're running a different one—the one that ends in irrelevance.

You Can't Compete Based on Who You Were

You are competing with what your customer expects next.

With the next best product, the next best story, the next best experience. That's the benchmark, and it keeps moving.

If your team's energy is directed at defending old strategies instead of trying new ones, it's time to reconsider what you're protecting.

Are you staying true to your core beliefs? Or just maintaining a comfort zone?

Because there is a difference.

Innovation Without Identity Is Just Noise

Change for the sake of change isn't the solution. Constantly shifting without a solid foundation makes your brand unpredictable and forgettable.

That's why everything you do—every iteration, every test, every bold move—must align with your brand's core identity.

Your purpose. Your promise. Your personality.

Evolution rooted in who you are adds energy. Change disconnected from that just causes confusion.

Understand the distinction.

Your People Feel It, Too

Standing still affects not only your customers but also your team.

When employees in your company feel that nothing is progressing, they lose interest. Curious minds become bored. Passionate people feel trapped. Momentum comes to a halt.

But when your brand evolves—when it stretches, experiments, and learns—your people feel that, too.

It generates energy. Alignment. Pride.

And people want to work for brands that make an effort.

Belief Doesn't Mean Blind Loyalty

Even your biggest fans won't stick around forever if they feel you've stopped caring, stopped growing, or stopped seeing them.

Belief is emotional, but it still carries expectations.

Customers want to believe that the brand they chose yesterday is still worth choosing tomorrow. That the things they loved are still present—and new things are being added to keep the relationship alive.

Complacency destroys that belief. Effort defends it.

What Now?

Ask the tough questions:

- Which part of our story needs refreshing?
- What's no longer connecting like it used to?
- Where are we lagging, and what's the price of remaining there?

Then act. Try. Learn. Improve. Most important, keep moving.

Because movement sends a message: We're still here. We're still evolving. We're still working hard to earn your belief.

The Heart of the Matter

- **Relevance is never permanent; it must be continuously re-earned.**
- **Progress doesn't need reinvention, but it does need purpose.**
- **Standing still doesn't protect your brand. It puts it at risk.**

Chapter 24
Brands That Lost Their Stand
They Failed to Adapt

BRANDS OFTEN DISAPPEAR LONG before they are officially declared dead. The signs are there—subtle at first, then more noticeable—until belief quietly fades away. What was once loved, trusted, and discussed becomes overlooked, irrelevant, or forgotten.

We like to think great brands are timeless icons, immune to decline. But they're not. They're living, evolving relationships. And like any relationship, they fade when neglected, ignored, or taken for granted.

Even the most beloved brands can falter if they forget what originally made people love them. When efficiency takes precedence over empathy, when the focus on short-term gains overrides long-term purpose, and when signs of cultural change are ignored, they risk losing their footing. Sometimes it's not outright failure but quiet erosion—where old habits overshadow new relevance until trust begins to fade.

This chapter isn't about failure just for failure's sake. It's about the quiet—and sometimes spectacular—ways brands lose their foothold. Some were giants. Some were disruptors. Some faded slowly; others collapsed seemingly overnight. All once mattered, until they didn't.

Here are a few that still echo in my mind. These are my perceptions of what almost or sadly did go wrong.

Kodak:
A Snapshot of Fear Over Foresight

For decades, Kodak was more than a brand—it was an emotional language. A "Kodak moment" didn't need explanation. It symbolized joy, connection, and memories.

But inside the company, things were falling apart. In 1975, Kodak created the first digital camera—then kept it hidden. Leadership was afraid it would threaten their profitable film business. Instead of adapting, they upheld the status quo and ignored their own innovation.

By the time they adopted digital technology, it was already too late. Smartphones had taken over. Social media had changed how people capture and share moments. Kodak still believed in the power of emotional storytelling—but had lost the means to deliver it.

This wasn't a case of market failure. It was a brand paralyzed by its own success. Kodak died on a hill of hesitation.

BlackBerry:
Essential to Essentially Obsolete

There was a time when carrying a BlackBerry on your hip signified importance. It represented power, efficiency, and connectivity. Its physical keyboard was legendary. Its encryption? Industry gold standard.

But as the smartphone era began, BlackBerry stuck to its traditional strengths—security, enterprise control, and the tactile keyboard—while ignoring what the mass market increasingly wanted: ease of use, elegance, apps, and flexibility.

Apple didn't just introduce a phone. It launched a lifestyle. Meanwhile, BlackBerry—slow to innovate and unify its software strategy—became a footnote.

Technological arrogance can be more damaging than ignorance. It leads you to believe you're right—until the world proves you're wrong.

AOL:
From Dominance to Falling Behind

"You've got mail." For many, that wasn't just a notification—it marked the start of a relationship with the internet.

AOL was more than just a portal; it was the gateway to a new digital lifestyle. However, its leadership confused distribution with loyalty. Broadband technology emerged. Platforms expanded. Still, AOL stayed the same.

Others shifted toward content ecosystems and personalization. AOL became bloated, ad-driven, and outdated. It stopped listening, and users stopped logging in.

Pandora:
Innovation Without a Distinct Identity

Before Spotify and Apple Music, there was Pandora—a clever recommendation engine with dedicated users and a first-mover advantage.

But that wasn't enough. Pandora's interface didn't evolve. Its heavily ad-supported approach frustrated users, and it never clearly defined itself beyond "radio, but smarter."

Meanwhile, Spotify built a community. Apple Music embraced culture. Both made music personal. Pandora became just a utility. You used it. But you didn't truly feel it.

In a world shaped by identity and emotion, being helpful isn't the same as being loved.

Starbucks:
Can the Giant Continue to Live Large and Maintain Its Cultural Leadership?

Starbucks built its empire not just on coffee but on culture. It turned getting a drink into a ritual and a place of refuge.

But in the 2000s, growth diluted its core. The experience felt scripted, baristas became replaceable, and stores lost their spirit.

Howard Schultz returned in 2008, refocused on craft and connection, and reignited belief. The brand evolved by embracing loyalty technology, mobile ordering, and even AI.

Yet challenges continue to surface. New coffee chains seem to emerge every year. Almost every street corner has an independent, entrepreneur-owned coffeehouse offering an alternative to giants like Starbucks. Ongoing labor unrest over pay, hours, and quality of life leads people to question whether these struggles compromise the values Starbucks once championed. As Starbucks moves toward automation, it's natural to wonder: Can a brand that grew through personal connection sustain that intimacy on a larger scale?

Bed Bath & Beyond:
Drowning in Deals

At its peak, Bed Bath & Beyond was the go-to store for every stage of life. Dorm rooms. Weddings. First apartments. It was part of the script.

But the script grew stale. Coupons became a crutch. Stores became cluttered. Online experiences lagged behind competitors.

Then came private equity, activist investors, cost reductions, and broken brand promises.

The brand didn't just become irrelevant—it gave up trying to defend itself.

RadioShack:
Curiosity Without a Cause

RadioShack was once the candy store for tech tinkerers: cables, components, and raw possibility.

But the future arrived, and RadioShack did not adapt. As electronics shifted from hobbyist parts to sleek consumer devices, it never found a new purpose. While Best Buy reinvented itself with a focus on service and expertise, and Amazon transformed convenience through e-commerce, RadioShack clung to an outdated model of selling cables, batteries, and components. It remained stuck in the past while the category—and the customer—moved forward.

Rebrands didn't succeed. Partnerships fell apart. And a new generation ignored it. RadioShack turned into a ghost—a reminder that relevance is earned every day.

Sears:
From Icon to Asset Sale

Sears was once the most iconic and innovative retailer in the US. Its catalog was extensive, and its stores served as community gathering places. Its private labels were trusted by many and considered equal to or better than national brands.

But Sears lost confidence in itself. Leadership stopped investing in innovation and instead focused on selling assets and cutting costs. Real estate was valued more than customers. Private equity priorities drained the experience—stores were stripped, inventory was reduced, and service deteriorated.

Customers didn't abandon Sears; Sears abandoned them first, sacrificing long-term loyalty for short-term cost savings.

When Efficiency Undermines Belief

One common theme in these stories is the relentless pursuit of efficiency and balance sheet savings, no matter the cost.

To an investor, a brand is an asset to be maximized. To a customer, a brand is a bond of trust.

The conflict between these two worldviews is where brand erosion begins. Reducing costs might improve short-term margins, but it can also weaken the emotional connection that originally built the trust. Advertising budgets decrease. Innovation comes to a halt. Culture is outsourced. Customers notice it—even if no spreadsheet can reveal it.

Leadership's Role, Especially in Private Equity

Many private equity firms acquire businesses primarily because of their strong brands—the recognition, trust, and emotional bonds built over decades.

But once inside, leadership encounters heavy pressure to deliver returns rapidly. One of the first areas to face funding cuts is marketing—the very engine that established that brand power.

This isn't an indictment of private equity—it's a leadership question. As a sponsor, how do you preserve and grow the value of the equity you've just invested in, while still enhancing operational performance?

The best investors understand that lowering costs can buy time, but building belief creates long-term value. Stewardship, not just spreadsheets, is what protects and grows the very thing you paid a premium to acquire.

Belief Doesn't Grow by Itself

What these brands lost wasn't just market share. It was relevance, resonance, and, most important, trust.

Belief is fragile. Once broken, it's hard to restore.

That's why I say: You can't save your way to strength. You can't cut your way to conviction. You can't outsource your reason for being.

Some brands never come back. But others—through clarity, courage, and humility—find their way back to what matters.

Those stories come next. The brands that didn't just survive a fall…but got back up.

The Heart of the Matter

- What warning signs are you ignoring?
- Every fallen brand once thought it was too iconic to fail. They didn't notice the erosion of belief until it was too late.
- Take a close look at where your relevance might be fading—customer trust, innovation, internal culture—and address it now.
- The safest brands aren't the largest or most vocal; they're the ones willing to acknowledge their vulnerabilities and act before belief is lost.

Chapter 25
The Reinventors
Brands That Adapt
and Endure

NOT EVERY BRAND THAT loses its way vanishes. Some return stronger—not because they stuck to their old ways but because leaders had the humility, clarity, and courage to evolve into something new.

Reinvention doesn't mean abandoning your past. It means reconnecting with what originally made you meaningful, then expressing that truth in the present—sometimes in ways that are uncomfortable or unfamiliar. It's about honoring your roots while building your relevance.

Reinvention requires leaders willing to take risks, face criticism, and sometimes even challenge shareholders or tradition. It demands a clear vision, tough decisions, and a readiness to be misunderstood. You might lose people along the way. But for brands that do it right, the reward is rare: a second act that feels as genuine—and sometimes even more effective—than the first.

Here are a few that didn't just survive change. They drove it.

Barbie:
Reinventing the Icon

For decades, Barbie was both cherished and controversial. She sparked imaginations—but also represented narrow beauty ideals. Over time, that imbalance became impossible to ignore.

Mattel could have preserved its legacy. Instead, it decided to reinvent it. Barbies now feature a variety of body types, skin tones, professions, and cultural backgrounds. Leadership listened and implemented changes.

Then came the 2023 film—a worldwide hit that celebrated Barbie while also exploring her legacy. It was meta, bold, and heartfelt. It united generations and reintroduced Barbie as a brand with both awareness and humor.

Barbie transformed from outdated to omnipresent, showing that reinvention can be both uplifting and joyful. It also proved that acknowledging past mistakes can deepen emotional connection.

Crocs:
From Joke to Juggernaut

Once just a punchline, Crocs were mocked more than they were marketed. Foam clogs didn't shout "cool." Yet beneath the ridicule, there was something real: comfort, utility, and uniqueness.

Instead of pulling back, Crocs leaned in. Leadership embraced irony and originality, working with high-fashion designers, pop stars, and influencers. They introduced customizable charms and limited editions.

They turned hate into hype. Mockery into momentum. Crocs became more than shoes—they became a cultural wink, a wearable symbol of rebellion.

Now, Crocs is a billion-dollar company with a fanbase that ranges from nurses to runway models. Reinvention didn't come from abandoning what made them unique—but from embracing it.

Abercrombie & Fitch:
Transitioning from Exclusion to Inclusion

Abercrombie built its brand in the early 2000s around exclusivity—shirtless models, dimly lit stores, and a cool-kid vibe that eventually became toxic. Its appeal was intentionally narrow. But times changed and the brand didn't.

Then came the reckoning—lawsuits, documentaries, public backlash. Most brands would have vanished into obscurity.

Abercrombie's ownership made a difficult decision. They restructured leadership, revamped the product line, and, most important, shifted the values—not just the image.

Today's Abercrombie embodies confidence, comfort, and inclusivity. The tone is more relaxed. The clothing is more practical. The audience is broader. It didn't just change its products; it changed what it represents.

LEGO:
Rediscovering the Magic

LEGO nearly lost its relevance as kids increasingly preferred screens, causing sales to decline and the brand to risk becoming a nostalgic memory.

Leadership avoided panic and fads. Instead, they focused on the brand's core: imagination and creation. LEGO expanded into movies, gaming, and adult fandoms. It partnered with franchises like Star Wars and Harry Potter, creating sets that felt like cultural statements.

Most important, LEGO listened. It learned from fans, fostered creativity, and started initiatives to support neurodiverse children. It turned childhood play into a lifelong passion.

By rediscovering its purpose, LEGO evolved from "just toys" into a symbol of curiosity for all ages.

Apple:
From Edge to Center

There was a time when Apple was struggling. The company created too many products without enough focus. Its brand lost significance.

Then Steve Jobs, who had previously been forced out of the company, returned. Instead of overwhelming the market with new features, he chose to simplify. He focused on clarity instead of clutter.

The "Think Different" campaign rekindled belief—not just through specs but through soul. Then came the iMac, iPod, and iPhone. Apple didn't just invent products—it shaped culture.

Even after the untimely death of Steve Jobs, leadership continued to evolve—shifting from hardware to software, from computers to wearables, from products to services. Apple today isn't just about what it makes; it's about what it represents.

McDonald's:
Reinventing the Familiar

You don't often think about reinvention when you see a Big Mac. But McDonald's has quietly evolved over the past decade.

It modernized menus, adopted digital drive-thrus, and partnered with cultural icons to stay relevant. Stores were redesigned, packaging was refreshed, and campaigns became more emotional, connecting with a new generation while keeping loyalty among existing customers.

McDonald's proved that even a well-established brand can stay flexible if leaders are willing to refresh its image while maintaining trust.

Harley-Davidson:
The Rebellion Rides On

For decades, Harley-Davidson embodied leather, grit, and Americana. But a new generation wasn't interested.

Leadership started evolving. Electrified models. Inclusive campaigns. A broader view of what freedom and rebellion look like.

It's still early, and balancing legacy with innovation can be tough. But Harley's leaders know that reinvention isn't about losing their identity—it's about growing who is part of it.

What Reinventors Do Right

These brands acknowledge their past. They learn from it—but they don't romanticize it.

Leaders make tough decisions before they are forced to. They don't wait for disruption—they create it. They listen. They adapt. They protect their core while transforming the edges.

Reinvention isn't reactive; it's reflective. It's driven by clarity, humility, and courage.

And at its core, it's emotional. Successful reinvention doesn't just restore competitiveness—it rebuilds belief. It grows alongside the audience. It stays culturally relevant. It risks disappointing purists to connect with more people.

Because branding isn't just about market share at its core. It's about meaning. It's about mattering. It's about having the courage to ask, "Are we still loved? Are we still needed?"—and taking bold action if the answer is no.

In the next chapter, we go even further. Beyond just surviving. Beyond just reinventing. To find out what it really takes for a brand to win a place in someone's heart.

The Heart of the Matter

- **Reinvention doesn't always mean starting over; it means rediscovering the courage to evolve while holding onto your core beliefs.**
- **Identify areas where you've been clinging to the past instead of creating the future.**
- **Reinvention begins with a brave step toward regaining relevance and confidence.**

Chapter 26
Share of Heart
Where Thinking Ends, Feelings Begin

WE'VE EXPLORED EMOTIONAL LOYALTY. We've explored belief.

Share of Heart is where those ideas come together.

Over the years, marketers have pursued share of mind, share of wallet, share of voice, and, more recently, share of algorithm. We've measured impressions, engagement, and sentiment. We've celebrated virality and volume. We've tracked clicks and conversions, calculated CAC (customer acquisition cost) and LTV (lifetime value), and convinced ourselves that loyalty could be modeled like a spreadsheet.

But the brands that last—those that aren't just selected but adored—gain something altogether different.

They earn the heart.

They earn space in someone's life. Not just as a helpful product but as a trusted presence. Not as noise in the feed but as a feeling. A memory. A relationship. A ritual.

That's Share of Heart, and it's the deepest kind of loyalty a brand can earn.

The Heart Is Emotional Real Estate

You don't earn a place in someone's heart by asking for it. You don't obtain it with a clever tagline or a discount code. You don't acquire it through targeting or scale it with automation.

You get there by showing up repeatedly as something worth believing in.

It's not about whether your campaign went viral. It's about whether someone thinks of you during a moment that matters. It's about whether they feel something when they see your name.

Do they reach for your product during nervous, celebratory, or comforting moments?

Do they associate you with a cherished memory or a version of themselves they're proud of?

Do they feel like your brand understands them—not just in a demographic sense but on a human level?

That's Share of Heart. It's not earned in a moment. It's earned over time—through small gestures, consistency, and emotional alignment.

Once you have it, everything changes. You're not just a brand; you're now part of someone's life.

It's More than a Preference. It's Identity.

A brand that gains Share of Heart becomes more than just a purchase—it becomes a symbol.

Customers don't just use you. They relate to you. They post about you, wear you, share you. They brag about their loyalty—not because they want a reward but because they feel connected.

You become a shorthand for how they want to be seen. You become a part of their story.

This is what distinguishes truly loved brands from those that are simply known. Because when your brand reflects their values, embodies their hopes, or brings them joy, you are no longer just a provider. You become a mirror. A companion.

That's why this work matters. That's why branding is more than just strategy. Because when you earn the heart, you don't just earn customers. You earn believers.

It Can't Be Faked or Forced

You can't hack your way into someone's heart, take shortcuts to love, or automate empathy.

Share of Heart is the result of choices—human, emotional, and intentional choices.

You earn it by treating people with respect and dignity. You keep it by following through on your promises with actions. You grow it when your values are reflected in how you act—not just in what you say.

And you risk it when you forget what initially mattered to people.

We often think of branding as what we tell the world. But Share of Heart is what people say when we're not in the room. It's what they carry with them — not in their wallets but in their memories.

It Emerges During Quiet Moments

You won't always notice it. You won't always be able to follow it. But you'll know it's there.

Share of Heart shows up when:

- A customer recommends you to a friend, not because you asked but because they genuinely want to.
- Someone uses your product during a family tradition—holiday meals, back-to-school routines, or new baby gifts.
- You become the "go-to" brand not just because of habit but because of trust.

- You make someone feel safe, seen, or understood in
  a way that surprises even them.

These aren't moments of conversion. They're moments of connection. Moments of meaning. Moments that no amount of media budget can buy.

It's What Protects You

Every brand, no matter how beloved, will make mistakes.

There will be missteps—bad headlines, product problems, leadership choices that don't succeed. What matters most is what happens afterward.

When you've earned someone's heart, they don't abandon you at the first sign of trouble. They pause, they wait, and they give you space to explain. They want to believe you'll make it right.

Because the relationship you've built matters to them. Because they've invested not just money but emotion.

That's why Share of Heart is so powerful.

It fosters resilience. It cultivates grace. It gives you the opportunity to try again.

Without it, trust is delicate. With it, trust can be restored.

Share of Heart Starts with Leadership

This isn't just a branding insight; it's a leadership philosophy.

Share of Heart begins at the top. It shows in how you treat your people, how you make decisions, and how you define success.

It's more than a marketing goal—it's a company-wide commitment to being worthy of belief.

When leaders prioritize long-term trust over quick wins…when they listen before they sell… when they foster a culture that respects the customer's humanity…that's when Share of Heart becomes possible.

And once it does, the brand becomes more than just a business. It becomes a force for connection, meaning, and belonging.

It's Slow...Until It's Not

Earning someone's heart doesn't happen overnight.

It begins small. A thoughtful message. An amazing experience. A moment of true understanding. Most people won't even realize it's happening.

And then, one day, they'll realize they feel something.

They'll trust you, advocate for you, forgive your mistakes. They'll see you not just as a brand they use but as one they believe in.

And when that happens, you won't have to chase them anymore. They'll be chasing you.

In a World of Distractions, This Is What Sets You Apart

In a marketplace filled with noise and uniformity, Share of Heart is the genuine differentiator.

Anyone can copy your product, undercut your price, or spoof your campaign. But no one can replicate how people feel about you.

That feeling—when it's earned—is the most defensible asset .

It turns a product into a presence. A moment into a memory. A customer into a believer.

And in the end, that's what really matters.

Share of Heart Is the Payoff

Everything we've discussed—from the stand you take to the values you live, from the culture you build to the trust you earn— has led up to this.

To this chapter, to this idea, to this moment.

Because Share of Heart isn't just a tactic, campaign, or KPI (key performance indicator).

It's a result of showing up, of doing the hard things well, and of proving over time that you're worthy of love, not just attention.

If a Brand Stand is what you fight for, then Share of Heart is what you live for.

That's how brands become loved, belief is built—and you become unforgettable.

The Heart of the Matter

This book wasn't written to sell a framework. It's not a playbook or a system. It's a conversation—between you and me, and between the brands we love and the people who love them back.

I've made plenty of mistakes. I've experienced great wins and tough misses. But if there's one thing I've learned, it's this:

- The most important place a brand can hold is in someone's heart.
- Not because it guarantees success but because it shows you mattered.
- If anything in these pages helped you see that more clearly, then it was worth writing.
- Keep showing up. Keep proving it. Keep earning belief.

Because once you've found your stand...and once you've earned Share of Heart...you don't just have a brand. You have a legacy.

Chapter 27
The Future of the Brand Stand
What Lies Ahead?

THIS ISN'T JUST A forecast; it's a clear call to action.

The next era of branding won't wait for cautious leaders or timid ideas. It won't reward noise without meaning or promises without proof. It will belong to the brave—those willing to stand for something greater than their product, profits, or even their success.

They won't create brands just to make noise; they'll create them to be treasured. They will not sell to consumers; instead, they will stand with believers. They won't compete for a share of the wallet; instead, they'll earn a Share of Heart.

Tomorrow's brands will not shout; they will resonate. They will not manipulate; they will matter. They will not chase clicks; they will foster a sense of belonging.

The future of branding isn't for those who are content with business as usual. It's for those ready to reject the old marketing rules—the ones focused on reach, frequency, and impressions—and instead embrace a new call to action. One that commits to lead with truth and craft content that evokes emotion, not just grabs attention. To prove its promises every single day. And to build brands people brag about because they truly feel something, not just because they were told to.

Algorithms won't drive the future of branding; it will be driven by courage, belief, and the refusal to stand still when the world demands conviction.

This is the Brand Stand of tomorrow. And it begins now—with you.

1. The Non-Negotiables

A future brand must be founded on convictions—principles so essential they cannot be compromised. These are not gentle guidelines. These are the battlegrounds of tomorrow's marketplace.

- **We will not confuse speed with meaning.** Fast wins attention; meaning earns loyalty.
- **We won't sacrifice trust for quick wins.** Revenue can be recovered, but integrity can't.
- **We will not confuse awareness with impact.** Being noticed isn't the same as gaining trust.
- **We do not see loyalty as a program.** Loyalty is built moment by moment, not through points and perks.
- **We will not misuse data.** We will use technology to help people, not to manipulate them.
- **We won't pretend to feel empathy.** Genuine caring isn't scripted; it's a promise.
- **We will not dilute our purpose to gain broader appeal.** A stand is only strong when it's not afraid to polarize.
- **We won't mistake a trend for a belief.** Purpose isn't just marketing; it's the essence of the brand.
- **We won't create for everyone.** We'll focus on those who share our beliefs.

Each of these non-negotiables has a cost. Living by them may mean turning down certain opportunities, not chasing every metric, and sometimes losing a sale today to gain a lifelong supporter. But there's no other way to build a brand that will matter tomorrow.

2. The Human Imperative

Technology will continue to accelerate, shaping every transaction, interaction, and experience. Algorithms will forecast our choices. AI will produce copy, design interfaces, and automate decisions we previously managed ourselves. But the one thing technology cannot do is care.

Tomorrow's brands will not out-code each other. They will out-care each other.

Imagine the future marketplace: A brand doesn't just know your purchase history; it understands your values, hopes, and fears. It greets you like an old friend—not because its CRM (customer relationship management) system is advanced but because its culture is.

We must prevent progress from eroding our humanity.

The brands that succeed will be those that understand that technology is a tool—not a substitute—for connection. The human imperative isn't optional; it's the foundation of every lasting brand of tomorrow.

3. The Leadership Pledge

The future will challenge leaders more than ever before. Markets will become more chaotic. Trust will become more fragile. Attention spans will decrease while expectations will rise rapidly. In that environment, leadership cannot remain neutral. It must take a stand.

The leader of tomorrow must guide with several crucial points of focus:

- **Lead with clarity.** Your team, customers, and community must always understand what you stand for and why you exist.
- **Lead with courage.** Choose conviction over convenience, even when the safer choice tempts you.

- **Protect trust.** Always prioritize long-term credibility over short-term gains.
- **Champion purpose.** A brand's reason for being will never be an afterthought; it will be its north star.
- **Be a guardian of belief.** Leadership's role isn't just to increase revenue but to cultivate the belief that breathes life into their brand.

4. The Future Brand Stand

Imagine a future marketplace where each brand truly represents something meaningful.

Where every product you buy tells a story you're proud to share. Where loyalty isn't manufactured—it's felt. Where marketing feels less like interruptions and more like inspiration.

These are not just distant possibilities—they are decisions we're making today.

The Brand Stand of tomorrow won't happen by chance. It will be earned by those willing to risk being different, to refuse to be everything to everyone, and to have the courage to take a stand.

Brands that take this stand will last because they are more than just a logo or campaign. They have become something bigger: a promise, a belief, a place where people see themselves reflected and valued.

The future won't wait. The question is, will you?

Throughout my career, I've collected a few reminders—simple truths that have guided me through tough decisions and brand battles. Think of them as a pocket-sized companion—the kind of thoughts I hope you might want to revisit from time to time.

In the next chapter, we'll examine some final reflections, including my "Warren-isms."

Chapter 28
Final Reflection
Warren-isms to Remember

IF THE PREVIOUS CHAPTERS covered strategy, then these Warren-isms are the sparks—hard-won truths, shorthand strategies, and quick reminders that have guided my career.

I didn't give my notes this title; others did. Over time, the people I've worked with started calling these one-liners and sharp truths "Warren-isms." Not because they belong solely to me but because they've become a key part of how I show up, how I coach, and how I cut through the clutter when it matters most.

My Warren-isms aren't about ego—they're about efficiency. These lines communicate ideas concisely and strike a chord. Some were spoken in pitch rooms, others were scribbled on napkins. My office wall was once filled with Post-it notes capturing these thoughts, each one earning its spot.

These aren't just quotes. They're living truths—shaped by experience, mistakes, and time. Use them as shorthand when things go sideways or meetings start drifting off track. Many already appear throughout this book. Some may be new to you.

Strategy First. Always.
Without a clear strategy, the creative process risks spiraling out of control. Tools and tactics are ineffective without a defined direction.

Branding Isn't Advertising, and Advertising Isn't Branding.

Strong branding is established well before advertising starts. Communication should support the brand, not create it.

A Brand Is a Promise, Made and Kept.

The most straightforward and powerful definition. Everything starts and finishes here.

When Your Message Is Clear, There's No Need to Shout.

Make your brand stand out—visually, verbally, and emotionally.

You Can't Boil the Ocean.

Picking your spots and setting priorities is the best way to chart your course to a strong Brand Stand. If you attempt to do too much too quickly, you risk everything falling apart.

Sort Through the Opinions to Clarify Your Purpose.

Any skilled management team benefits from diverse opinions. Leadership involves listening, learning, then establishing a clear direction.

Loyal Customers Select Brands They Feel Connected With.

Understand this, and your entire branding approach changes.

If They Feel It, They'll Share It.

Emotions drive advocacy. Build resonance, and you expand your reach.

Humanity Isn't Just a Strategy— It's a Superpower.

Especially in uncertain times, being human beats being clever.

Technology Empowers. Humanity Connects.

Use technology to enable—not replace—human connection.

The Best Marketers See Themselves As Irrelevant.

You're rarely the target audience. Understand and listen to your customers. Get out of the way.

Don't Just Tell Me You're Funny— Make Me Laugh.

Claims are meaningless without proof. Let people feel it.

Trust Is Built Quietly; It Is Broken Loudly.

Every small proof matters; every broken promise leaves a mark.

Marketing That Rewards Attention Builds Business.

Connection over volume wins in a noisy world.

Data Is Invaluable, but It Doesn't Replace Sound Judgment.

Knowledge matters, but knowing how—and when—to apply it matters more.

Know Your Brand Before Hiring the Experts.

Belief must come from within. No agency can fake it for you.

Culture Eats Strategy. But Brand Feeds Culture.

Internal belief shapes external trust. Alignment is non-negotiable.

You Can't PowerPoint Your Way to Purpose.

Purpose isn't a slide—it's a decision. Live it.

Marketing Isn't Magic, but Great Marketing Feels Magical.

When it works, it's more than awareness—it's belief.

Brands That Succeed Aren't Just Different; They're Decisive.

Indecision kills momentum. Clarity builds conviction.

The Best Ideas Often Feel Risky at First.

True progress causes discomfort. That's how you know you're pushing boundaries.

Detail, Detail, and More Detail

Every small detail matters—signage, scent, tone, lighting. Little cues leave big impressions.

The Best Branding Doesn't Just Announce Itself; It Proves Itself.

Proof comes from consistent actions and execution.

Brand Equity Is Earned, Not Given.

It's a contract with customers that needs to be renewed continuously.

You Seldom Get a Second Chance to Make a First Impression.

Decisions are made quickly and are difficult to undo.

If Everything Is Important, then Nothing Truly Is.

Great brands prioritize focus over noise.

Nostalgia Can Buy Time but Not a Future.

Relevance—rather than history—determines what comes next.

If You Stay Still, You're Likely to Fall Behind.

Customers drift away when you don't evolve.

Constantly Expand the Circle of Belief.

Attract, serve, go above and beyond, stay relevant, and watch the circle of belief expand.

No Brand Is Invulnerable.

Thinking you're invincible is the first step toward losing touch.

You Don't Need to Be the Smartest Person in the Room.

You don't want to be. Great leaders surround themselves with talent and empower it.

Maestro, Please! Lead Like a Conductor.

Leadership is like conducting a symphony—individual brilliance only matters when it works in harmony.

Brand-Building Is a Team Sport.

Create a solid game plan. Select the right players. Allow them to execute with each knowing their role.

My Final Note About Warren-isms

Feel free to underline these, post them, or quote them. But more important, live them. Because the best brands aren't built with the biggest budgets.

They're built with belief.

Closing Note

IF YOU'VE MADE IT this far, thank you.

This wasn't written to be a textbook or even to provide a formula; it was written as a reflection, a conversation, a collection of hard truths and optimistic reminders gathered from decades of building brands that matter.

You've heard my stories, my shorthand, my convictions. But this isn't about my voice.

It's about yours.

What will you learn from this? How will you apply it to your brand, team, or next big idea?

Because none of this matters if it stays on the page. Brands don't exist in decks; they exist in decisions.

So, take these notes from the shelf and bring them into the room. Share them in the product roadmap, the pitch, the customer moment, and the hallway conversation.

Make them yours. Please bring them to life.

And remember: You don't need to be loud to get noticed. You don't have to be big to make a difference. You don't need to be perfect to earn trust.

All you need to do is care.

And if you genuinely do—really do—people will notice.

That's the way brands develop, trust is built, and belief is established.

Thank you to the brands mentioned throughout this book. These reflections are based on public actions, campaigns, and my interpretations. They are offered with admiration, not affiliation.

And to you, the reader, thank you for dedicating your time, attention, and perhaps even your heart to these ideas.

Now go make it matter.

—Warren

Index

About the Author

WARREN KORNBLUM has dedicated his career to helping brands build trust and belief, not just attract attention. From Clio Award-winning ad campaigns to global brand makeovers, he combines a unique blend of creative intuition and leadership in every brand he partners with.

Known for emphasizing his belief in Share of Heart—the idea that the most meaningful brands are the ones that earn emotional loyalty—Warren has advised start-ups and Fortune 500 companies alike, always returning to the same truth: Branding isn't just about what you say—it's about how you behave.

He started his career in advertising, producing campaigns that received praise from the industry. Later, he sold his agency to Bozell Worldwide, where he took on the role of managing partner of Bozell Retail. There, he led strategic and creative efforts for major global consumer brands.

Warren later became the chief marketing officer of Toys "R" Us, helping to reshape one of the most iconic retail brands of its time. He then served as chief strategy officer at Rooms To Go and later as senior advisor to the CEO and chief marketing officer of Serta Simmons Bedding, playing a key role in guiding brand and business strategy during critical moments of change.

Today, Warren advises boards, shareholders, founders, and executive teams on building emotionally impactful and consistent brands. He is also deeply involved in philanthropic organizations, strongly believing that giving back is essential to giving both a brand and a life their true purpose.

This book highlights not only the strategies he developed but also the lessons he has learned.

www.ingramcontent.com/pod-product-compliance
Lightning Source LLC
Chambersburg PA
CBHW070758160726
48004CB00001B/238